MW00573431

P.O.V.

THE EIGHT PERSPECTIVES OF FICTION

P.O.V.

THE EIGHT PERSPECTIVES
OF FICTION

BY KRISTIN S. SMITH

NEW DEGREE PRESS
COPYRIGHT © 2021 KRISTIN S. SMITH
All rights reserved.

P.O.V.
The Eight Perspectives of Fiction

ISBN   978-1-63730-707-6   *Paperback*
              978-1-63730-798-4   *Kindle Ebook*
              979-8-88504-008-2   *Ebook*

Table of Contents

To Randy and Denise,

Who knew two conversations could lead to something so big?

Author's Note

My older brother Randy is thirteen years older than I am. As anyone with a large age gap between them and their sibling can tell you, it can be difficult to find shared interests, so you can imagine my excitement when I found out he not only likes to write but also favors the first-person point of view. We spent an hour talking about writing craft and the strengths of our preferred narration approach, and I loved every minute of it. After we hung up the phone, I immediately dialed my best friend Denise to tell her the good news: Randy and I shared a perspective!

She let me wear myself out, chattering about my conversation with my brother, before she asked me why I cared so much about which point of view he uses. She understood my excitement about sharing a hobby but didn't see the buzz behind the approach. I was five minutes into my impromptu lecture on the perks of first-person POV when Denise asked me this pivotal question: If it is so great, why does anyone use the other perspectives?

I gave Denise my initial thoughts (third if you want to make it feel like a movie and second if you want it to be a little unsettling) and was surprised by my lackluster response. I had spent so much time investing in my favorite perspective that I had ignored the others. Dissatisfied by my shallow comments, I promised Denise that I'd research the strengths and subcategories of the other points of view then get back to her with a more thorough answer, and well, here it is.

During the years since this conversation, I have been compiling my research, insights, and findings and their applications into an informative guide. This project has expanded from a report on my favorite narration types to a text that analyses each perspective in equal measure to help both novice and experienced writers navigate our craft more efficiently. POV is one of the core storytelling elements that dictate a work's reception, so it is essential that writers have a clear understanding of the available approaches to narration and its effects. My book aims to give creatives this information by defining each subsection of the three perspective categories and providing classic and contemporary literary examples.

How to Use This Book

——

This book is meant to inform readers about the properties, components, advantages, and disadvantages of the different writing perspectives based on my experiences and those of my fellow authors. This book can be read in order, or you can skip around depending on what you want to accomplish, so here are my suggestions for reading *P.O.V.*:

TEACHERS AND WRITING COACHES

If you're interested in teaching your students about the academic and artistic strengths of POV, this is the book for you! This project is first and foremost an educational tool. I structured *P.O.V.* like a textbook so that it's an easily navigable and intuitive reference. Each chapter defines a different perspective and breaks down its usage via written lectures and essays on popular classic novels and short stories.

P.O.V.'s chapters are ordered according to the narrator's scope to show how their proximity to the plot affects the story's delivery. The further out we get from the protagonist's head, the more information we're given. Like any textbook, each section prepares you for the next. I recommend reading it in order to get the full effect, though if you choose not to, I won't tell!

WRITERS AND CURIOUS READERS

No matter your genre of preference, this book is a useful tool to have in your arsenal. If you're interested in strengthening your grasp on a certain perspective, I recommend starting with your favorite. Each chapter walks you through the pros and cons of your preferred POV, so if you want a quick tune-up, take a gander at the table of contents, then make a beeline to wherever you want to be.

Inversely, if you are interested in improving your overall writing skills, I encourage you to start reading from the POV that you dislike the most and work your way to your favorite. This approach may seem unappealing, but I've personally found it useful. While working on this project, I went out of my way to use my least favorite points of view (second person and third omniscient), and my grasp of the two improved exponentially within a short timeframe.

Stepping out of my comfort zone forced me to pay more attention to my diction and the different ways the narrators allowed me to characterize my protagonists. As a serial first-person penman, I had settled in my formula for designing and developing characters, so once I removed myself from my preferred perspective, I began to seek out new approaches that not only helped me with my least favorite points of view but also innovated my writing when I returned to my favorite style. Hopefully, by forcing yourself outside of your comfort zone as I did, you will yield similar results.

FOR ALL THE ABOVE

As mentioned before, there is no one way to approach this book. The chapters feed into one another, but they can stand alone. The only thing that I strongly recommend you do first to get the most out of this book is to read the *Incipience* information. The before-and-after scope analyses are centered around the book's characters and plot, so you won't really get how the story has changed if you don't know what it was in the first place. Do yourself a favor and skim through the *Incipience* SparkNotes section so you can see just how much scope can shape a narrative!

Getting to Know
Incipience

PLOT SUMMARY

Many of the fiction excerpts of this book come from my novel *Incipience* (publishing date TBD). *Incipience* follows an eighteen-year-old Virgin Islander named Charlotte-Amalie "Mali" Joseph as she struggles to assimilate into an alien culture without abandoning her moral code in the process.

The summer Mali graduates from high school, Earth is struck by a series of meteors that contain poisonous chemicals. These compounds pollute the air, causing widespread illness and thousands of deaths. The planet spends two months in distress, too weak and technologically inept to neutralize the lingering contamination. During this time, Inovarians, an alien race of humanoids, make first contact with the United Nations and offer to repair the polluted atmosphere in exchange for young adults to help fight a war they are on the cusp of losing. The UN readily accepts their terms, and the contamination is cleared.

Incipience's protagonist, Mali, is one of the youths selected for this exchange. She tries to resist capture, so the Inovarians sedate her. For the next few hours, our protagonist is down, but she certainly isn't out. Mali's body adapts to reject the sedatives. The ship's scientists try to put her back under, but it's no use. Her prolonged exposure to chemicals has morphed her genome, making her immune to foreign agents.

The meteors that hit Earth contained compounds that weakened, killed, and in rare cases, mutated people. Mali, one of the select few, now has a rapid healing rate and hypersensitive reflexes that allow her to fight well. The Inovarians capitalize on her resilience and prowess by placing her in decorated Commander H'Jemrom "Rombag" Bagzah's cadet squadron. The two are at odds from the moment they meet, constantly arguing over the morality and necessity of war.

Mali is a self-proclaimed pacifist who doesn't mind a fistfight. She's willing to act in self-defense but is resolutely against causing lasting harm to another person. Battle-hardened Rombag, on the other hand, argues that you can't always pick your battles, but you surely have to fight them, despite your preferences. Their disagreement is only resolved when the Quinzentenians ambush their ship.

Mali's sense of self-preservation leads her to fight back, drawing comfort from the fact that she's only participating to survive. Her mindset is slowly tainted as the teen witnesses the Quinzentenians incapacitate her team. As the scene progresses, Mali's actions start to reflect her budding animosity. *Incipience*'s narration style focuses on this emotional journey, but there is so much more happening in this battle that affects the plot beyond the protagonist's individual experience.

I chose scenes from *Incipience* to show how a work's perspective changes its literary interpretations. As you re-read the *Incipience* portions through each chapter, you'll learn more about the moving pieces of the scene that Mali is blind to and learn how POV dictates the reading and writing experience.

PART 1
THE INTERNAL: KEEP YOUR READERS CLOSE AND YOUR NARRATORS CLOSER

Authors choose their story's point of view according to their desired effect. They use second and third-person narrators to give readers an aerial view of the plot's events, while the first-person perspectives put us on the ground with the protagonist.

These accounts are rooted in the character's emotions and move us to empathize with them as they overcome obstacles, foster new relationships, and grow as a person. First-person texts possess a diary-like intimacy because they give us access to the narrator's innermost thoughts, feelings, and secrets from the first page to the last. This information draws readers into the plot since after a few pages, the protagonist starts to feel like a new friend we're getting to know.

Some authors favor third-person narrators because they prefer to capture their stars with a wider lens. Those speakers do an excellent job unfolding plots with clever foreshadowing and well-timed head-hops, but they lack the sensationalism that the first person provides. Many people love being immersed in the protagonist's life and cling to works that allow them such riveting proximity to their favorite characters. This relationship will keep readers coming back for more, so in the spirit of keeping your audience close, take a closer look at the perks of the first-person points of view before writing them off.

First-Person Protagonist POV

———

Just as a car collector never forgets their first Porsche, an author never forgets their first big project. I started writing when I was eleven at the request of my friend Stacie. She loved the short stories I'd throw together for class, so she badgered me for weeks on end to draft something for her. I was initially reluctant because while I enjoyed toying with the prompts our teachers gave us, I frankly wasn't sure if I had the creative capacity to produce an original work. Stacie, God bless her persistent soul, insisted that I could and told me to have a chapter in her hand by the next week or else she'd ramp up her nagging. Already irritated and afraid of what she'd do when she was really trying to get under my skin, I got to typing.

It took a while to figure out what to do, but with some inspiration from Ally Carter's Gallagher Girls series (a childhood favorite of mine that I stand by to this day), I came up with "Addison Academy," an admittedly raggedy spy book about a teenage girl named Amber and her ragtag group of

BFFs. This project was essentially an extensive Gallagher Girl fan fiction that was one plot hole away from being certified Swiss cheese, but man, was it a memorable first.

Inspired by Carter's series, I narrated "Addison Academy" in the first-person protagonist point of view, a choice that made the writing experience addicting. This perspective had me in a vice grip because it allowed me to feel like I was a part of the action. While I was physically tethered to my computer, my keyboard allowed me to tour my fictional world to solve mysteries, battle bad guys, and narrowly dodge close calls alongside Amber. With each new adventure, I learned more about my character, writing craft, and most remarkably, myself.

As many novice writers (juvenile or otherwise) do, I inserted an *embarrassing* amount of my personality, mannerisms, fears, hopes, and dreams into Amber until she became an idealized version of myself. I used her as an avenue to explore who I was, who I wasn't, and who I wanted to be. Ten years later, my novels are no longer my primary personality workshop space, but my first-person experiences with Amber have a special place in my heart because they showed me just how immersive and insightful the perspective can be.

DEFINITION

Works told in the first-person protagonist (FPP) point of view are narrated by the story's central character (also known as the protagonist, hence the POV's name). This narration style uses first-person pronouns (I, me, my, etc.) to describe what is happening from the character's perspective. The FPP POV allows readers to view the character's thoughts and feelings as they navigate through the story.

This perspective limits viewers to the protagonist's thoughts, feelings, and experiences, essentially leaving us blind to everything beyond the character's immediate knowledge. Some people dislike this tunnel vision-esque point of view because they can only traverse the plot through the narrator's limited scope and biased lens. Inversely, many readers (like yours truly) enjoy the immersive nature of the FPP perspective because it feels like they're almost the character or a close friend privy to the figure's private thoughts.

The FPP POV is arguably the most useful perspective for making people form an instantaneous connection with the protagonist. It gives us access to the character's innermost thoughts from the beginning of the work, and this intimate knowledge leads us to form an immediate (and oftentimes lasting) bond with them. We get front row tickets to their lives as they develop across arcs, overcome obstacles, and meet milestones, so it's hard not to feel attached to them by the end of the book.

Though utilized across genres, the FPP narration style is heavily associated with romance and coming-of-age stories because they fixate on emotional sentiments and relationships. The audience's fondness of the protagonist makes the figure's successes, sorrows, highs, and lows resonate more deeply than the other perspectives do because the audience is intimately involved with the character's development from the first page. Take John Green's *The Fault in Our Stars,* for example.

Anyone old enough to remember the rise of *TFIOS* can attest to tweenagers' personal investment in Green's leading lady, Hazel Grace Lancaster. I remember talking about Hazel with my classmates as if she were someone we personally knew. During first period, I would gripe about the protagonist's irrational decisions—seriously, who makes out with their boyfriend at the Anne Frank Museum?—and at lunch, my friend Megan and I would mourn with Hazel over her (spoiler alert!) boyfriend's tragic passing.

When the book hit the screens in 2014, there wasn't a dry eye at the premiere—even *before* anything sad happened. Fans were already heavily invested in Hazel's journey after living in her head for so long, so seeing a physical representation of her pain hurt all the more. Green understood the power of this perspective and wielded it well, as many a (early) Generation Z tween/teen YA romance fan can attest to.

PERSPECTIVE ATTRIBUTES

SENSATIONALISM

The first-person perspective is *sensational*. It's thrilling, intimate, enthralling, entertaining, and most importantly, it's what *you* make it. Just like everything else sensual (i.e., appealing to the five senses), your audience's reaction is dependent on their experience. As an author, it's your job to lure people into your plot and give them a reason to stay. Readers are motivated to stick around when they (a) connect with the protagonist(s) and (b) have a thorough understanding of the setting. The perspective best suited for both is the FPP POV.

The FPP POV is perfect for making quick connections between the readers and the protagonist. The same can be said for world-building. While the other perspectives are arguably better for giving a holistic overview of what a setting looks like, the FPP POV is the best for knowing what a world *feels* like.

As residents in the protagonist's head, readers experience the sensationalism of a new space alongside the character. The audience can nearly feel the textures, hear the background noise, taste the described flavors, and smell the scents, and they can most definitely picture each scene in their mind's eye as the narrator describes it.

The FPP POV sells readers a sense of wonder and excitement that the other perspectives can't reach. For example, an astronaut's first steps on Mars would be a lot more riveting through their eyes rather than a second or third-person narrator because these other perspectives would be too removed from the story for the prose to narrate as well. While the two could tell us what occurred, the astronaut's FFP account would make us *feel* the moment. The character's language would be shaped by their unique quirks, candid reactions, interesting insights, and novel discoveries, which would give us a much more personal and exciting story.

WORLD BUILDING

Every FFP scene has the propensity to be an exhilarating adventure because there's so much for readers to learn alongside the narrator. This is one of the many reasons that the FPP POV is perfect for stories that take place in extraordinary worlds that are unlike our own. Readers can easily get lost in the intricate social rules, complicated technology, and astounding geographic features of fictional worlds, but this perspective makes them easier to navigate.

The FPP POV has a limited scope, meaning that the narrator doesn't know or see everything about their setting or situation. The readers, who possess the same knowledge as the protagonist, are able to learn about the world gradually, making the nuances of each setting less overwhelming and easier to commit to memory. This perspective is especially useful when exploring the territories and cultures of a newly introduced world. As the narrator interacts with the different locations of a story, we're able to make sense of the setting and how it operates in an organic manner rather than getting an info dump in the exposition, a narrative method that can be dull to readers even if it is extremely useful.

The first-person protagonist point of view is also a great choice for authors who want to integrate unique elements into their stories, such as custom-made languages or intricate rituals. For example, throughout *Incipience*, Charlotte-Amalie "Mali" Joseph learns Inovarian, the language of the aliens she is traveling with. Her initial lack of communication skills serves as both frustration and motivation since it pushes her to expand her understanding of the aliens' language and the cultural practices associated with it. As Mali picks up bits of Inovarian, my readers do, too.

This approach not only allows my audience to gradually learn the language but also helps them to connect with the setting. The more familiar and accessible Inovarian is, the more tangible the aliens themselves become. The first-person protagonist POV is great for learning about a world, but it goes to say that if it isn't used properly, it can be an irritating rather than an immersive experience for readers. Just as the narrators in this perspective can be very tunnel-visioned, so can the authors if they don't pay close attention to their use of details.

After spending so much time building their world, some authors can forget that their character isn't an extension of themselves, especially since they're using first-person pronouns and internal dialogue to compose the story. This mistake often leads to plot holes and confusion because the protagonist has a disproportionate amount of insight into the story's mechanics. Inversely, some writers leave out chunks of key details because they are operating on their own fore-knowledge and assumptions rather than accounting for what their audience should logically know.

The first-person protagonist POV is all about the experiences, adventures, and connections that authors can provide readers, so it's important for us to balance the informational and sensational aspects of our works to excite and educate our audience while using this immersive perspective.

"The Cask of Amontillado"

———

"I resolved to diversify, and so heighten, the effect, by adhering, in general, to the monotone of sound, while I continually varied that of thought: that is to say, I determined to produce continuously novel effects . . ."

—EDGAR ALLAN POE, "THE PHILOSOPHY OF COMPOSITION"

"The Cask of Amontillado" (1846) by Edgar Allan Poe is one of my all-time favorite short stories because the narrator, a noble Frenchman named Montresor, is such a cheeky and dramatic character. Poe's protagonist kicks off his story with a declaration of vengeance for Fortunato, an Italian "friend" and wine connoisseur who committed an unpardonable— and more importantly, unspecified—sin against Montresor.

Our narrator does his absolute best to emphasize to his audience that Fortunato's offense consisted of a "thousand injuries" that require him to "not only punish but punish with impunity" yet ironically forgets to mention any particular "unredressed" wrongs Fortunato has committed. Nowhere in "The Cask of Amontillado" does Montresor explicitly list the transgressions that drive him to homicide, so readers are as clueless as Fortunato with regard to what the Italian did to warrant a death sentence.

All we know is that the narrator will be avenged by the end of the story and that Fortunato, for some reason, rightfully has it coming. This passion and precision differential is a perfect example of the first-person protagonist POV's tunnel-visioned nature.

> The thousand injuries of Fortunato I had borne as I best could; but when he ventured upon insult, I vowed revenge. You, who so well know the nature of my soul, will not suppose, however, that I gave utterance to a threat. At length I would be avenged; this was a point definitively settled—but the very definitiveness with which it was resolved, precluded the idea of risk. I must not only punish but punish with impunity. A wrong is unredressed when retribution overtakes its redresser. It is equally unredressed when the avenger fails to make himself felt as such to him who has done the wrong.
>
> It must be understood, that neither by word nor deed had I given Fortunato cause to doubt my good will. I continued, as was my wont,

to smile in his face, and he did not perceive that my smile now was at the thought of his immolation.

As guests in the protagonist's head, readers are given full access to the character's emotional journey throughout the plot, but it's important to note that we're not always guaranteed the full background information behind their motivation. Montresor's failure to communicate Fortunato's alleged sins shows not only the plot holes that can occur when using the FPP POV, but it also highlights how easily readers can disconnect from a character's quest because we lack the information needed to empathize with them.

It is important for writers to keep track of what they want us to know, what we need to know, and what reaction they want us to have to the characters' actions. If Montresor were to pause to explain what "wrong [that] is unredressed," more people may view his vengeance quest as a morally ambiguous yet worthy cause rather than petty premeditated murder. As is, the vast majority of readers oppose the narrator's actions but stay along for the ride to see where Montresor's twisted enthusiasm, theatrics, and cheeky comments take him.

My favorite aspect of "The Cask of Amontillado" is the dramatic irony created from the contrast between Montresor's internal dialogue and his actions. Like all other first-person protagonist narrators, the Frenchman's internal commentary reveals his genuine intentions as he interacts with others. This vantage point allows us to see the disparities between what he says, does, and thinks.

The contrast between the narrator's motives and actions is especially entertaining in the case of morally murky protagonists like Montresor. Despite his charming, well-mannered demeanor, Poe's protagonist has nothing but sinister intentions for his "friend." The Frenchman goes to great lengths to pretend that he cares for Fortunato so that the inebriated Italian doesn't suspect his betrayal until the very end.

> He had a weak point—this Fortunato—although in other regards he was a man to be respected and even feared. He prided himself on his connoisseurship in wine. Few Italians have the true virtuoso spirit. For the most part their enthusiasm is adopted to suit the time and opportunity—to practise imposture upon the British and Austrian *millionaires*. In painting and gemmary, Fortunato, like his countrymen, was a quack—but in the matter of old wines he was sincere. In this respect I did not differ from him materially: I was skilful in the Italian vintages myself, and bought largely whenever I could.

> It was about dusk, one evening during the supreme madness of the carnival season, that I encountered my friend. He accosted me with excessive warmth, for he had been drinking much. The man wore motley. He had on a tight-fitting parti-striped dress, and his head was surmounted by the conical cap and bells. I was so pleased to see him, that I thought I should never have done wringing his hand.

In the short story's exposition, ever-friendly Fortunato "accosted [the narrator] with excessive warmth, for he had been drinking much." Montresor is giddy to see the Italian in such a vulnerable state because his victim is now far more gullible than he otherwise would've been. The Frenchman tells Fortunato, a vintage wine expert, that he needs a consultation on the cask of Amontillado he has stored in his family's catacombs.

The drunk is, of course, enthused at the idea of sampling more wine, but he's downright insistent on helping him once Montresor says he's considering consulting Luchesi, a lesser wine taster that "cannot tell Amontillado from Sherry." Fortunato then "possesse[s] himself of [the narrator's] arm" and drags the Frenchman to where the wine was allegedly stored, a proactive action that makes him feel like he is in control when he is really being baited into a trap.

> He turned towards me, and looked into my eyes with two filmy orbs that distilled the rheum of intoxication.
>
> "Nitre?" he asked, at length.
>
> "Nitre," I replied. "How long have you had that cough?"
>
> "Ugh! ugh! ugh!—ugh! ugh! ugh!—ugh! ugh! ugh!—ugh! ugh! ugh!—ugh! ugh! ugh!"
>
> My poor friend found it impossible to reply for many minutes.
>
> "It is nothing," he said, at last.
>
> "Come," I said, with decision, "we will go back; your health is precious. You are rich, respected, admired, beloved; you are happy, as once I was. You are a man to be missed. For me it is no matter. We will go back; you will be ill, and I cannot be responsible. Besides, there is Luchesi—"

"Enough," he said; "the cough is a mere nothing; it will not kill me. I shall not die of a cough."

"True—true," I replied; "and, indeed, I had no intention of alarming you unnecessarily—but you should use all proper caution. A draught of this Medoc will defend us from the damps."

Every time I reread this short story, I am both in awe of and entertained by Montresor's master manipulation. Throughout this work, he not only makes himself seem like the passive character, but he also seamlessly slips into a kind and compassionate persona, an astonishing feat considering his vengeful nature and murderous intent. I find it very humorous how frequently Montresor pauses to check on Fortunato and feign concern for the tipsy fellow's health as he actively plots the man's demise. The funniest instance of this, in my opinion, is when Fortunato breaks out into a coughing fit.

Montresor states that they should leave the damp catacombs because Fortunato is "a man to be missed...and [Montresor] cannot be responsible" if something were to happen to the Italian in his care. To this, Fortunato replies that a cough wouldn't kill him, and Montresor enthusiastically agrees. I remember being floored with laughter at this interaction the first time I read "The Cask of Amontillado" because only readers, who are in tune with the narrator's thoughts, understand the true meaning of his words. This short story is littered with similar ironic displays of affection that make this a work of comedic *gold*.

"The Cask of Amontillado" is truly only as memorable as it is because of its narration style. There's nothing particularly novel about an unsuspecting betrayal story—we've been hearing variations of those since Cain and Abel's era—but Poe's choice of perspective makes his work stand out among the masses.

Montresor's theatrics would have been lost to readers had Poe told this short story in the third-person limited or omniscient point of view. A third-person limited perspective would have likely created an air of dramatic suspense surrounding the murder, and the third omniscient POV would have explored Fortunato's thoughts, humanizing him just enough for the work to qualify as a tragedy. Narrated as is, readers get to have fun watching Montresor's devious plan unfold without any of the anxiety typically attached to murder stories of this sort.

The first-person protagonist perspective is perfect for exploring conventionally villainous characters like Montresor because it gives readers insights into mindsets they may have never ventured. Actions speak louder than words when analyzing most characters, but thoughts tell more truths than any gesture or decision ever could. The contrast between Montresor's plotting and performative kindness shows how comical and enlightening introspective looks at characters can be.

Excerpt from *Incipience*

—

Rombag drafted me from the Pagi unit to the Izedi team because he values my specific skill set, but I wish he'd left me where I was. The Izedi's formation is flawless, their movements synchronized, and their extensive armor training make them the best team to back Rombag.

This group is comprised of the fifteen highest scoring cadets in our barrack of one hundred and twenty-five humans. I doubt they'll need much help, but the Pagis? My team of twenty-five—well, twenty-four now that I'm gone—can fight well, but they lack the prowess the Izedis have. My abilities could be the lifesaving buffer they need, yet I'm here with the golden group.

I divert my thoughts from my team and focus on the people I'm marching with now. It takes a few tries, but I'm able to find a place for myself at the rear of their diamond formation. The sound of our synchronized footfalls would have been soothing if we weren't heading toward the enemy.

We've been training to fight the Quinzentenians for months, but running a simulation is different than charging into battle. The only things keeping me level-headed right now are the sureness of Rombag's demeanor, my determination to survive, and the confidence radiating off of the Izedi squad.

Despite his laundry list of flaws, I can't help but respect Rombag's leadership skills. He's stayed on our comms, feeding us bits of praise and encouragement in the midst of his warnings and corrections. The team's morale surprisingly hasn't taken a drop. It's gone up since leaving the armory if anything.

What really impresses me isn't his pep talks, it's his willingness to draw fire. Our commander is always the first one to enter every room and corridor despite what Inovarian protocol typically calls for. According to our training, we're supposed to send a few sacrificial lambs in while he takes out the baited threat instead of the other way around. Not only that but he stands tall in the middle of the room while the rest of us stay low and complete our tasks. Anyone with sense would go for him first since he's the easiest target with the most embellishments on his uniform.

Why bother with a few pawns when you can secure an instant checkmate?

Rombag signals for us to halt. We reach the mess hall without seeing another soul. The route he gave the other teams should have pushed the Quinzentenians here, so for there to be no word from the other squadrons or any sign of the enemy makes my hair stand on end.

The Izedis relax not long after we secure the perimeter. Some murmur amongst themselves, asking whether or not this is an actual threat or just an intense drill. I can't help but shake my head. Do they honestly think every Inovarian would be on such high alert if this was one of Rombag's glorified pop quizzes?

I break away from my position against the wall and approach Rombag. Something about this calm lull feels wrong, and I have this burning itch that tells me we need to leave *immediately.* "Commander, something's not right. I think we should g—"

I feel the shot coming before I see it.

I hit the floor immediately, tackling Rombag down with me. A sickening *crack!* sounds out from above me. I don't pause long enough to let the impact register. I quickly roll off him, draw my pistol, and fire in the direction the laser came from.

My body hums with adrenaline. There's a threat in our presence, that much is obvious from the officer lying at my feet; the problem is that there's nothing in *sight.* Lasers fire off from all over the room, and within seconds, cadets are writhing on the floor. The rest of us shoot back in the general direction of where the discharges come from with no luck. Even though we're currently at a disadvantage, I'm at least grateful they're not going for kill shots like they were with . . . ROMBAG!

A pang of guilt strikes my conscious. I haven't even checked if he's alive. I turn to see the Inovarian slowly rising to his feet. His helmet, which I thought was impenetrable, is shattered beyond belief. Every inch of the black glass was crumpled by the force of the blast that, by the looks of it, hit him square in the forehead.

I scramble to help him up the rest of the way. "Commander, are you okay?"

Rombag gives me a mute nod as he unholsters his blaster.

My brows wrinkle, but the expression goes unseen behind my mask. Helmet or not, he should be at least a little rattled.

Is he actually alright, or is he just acting tough? I open my mouth to voice my concerns when a laser whizzes past me. I take a leap back, glad the floor's the one that's scorched and not me. Even with my rapid healing factor, I can still feel pain, and that definitely would have hurt. I draw my weapon again. Guess I'll have to question him later.

I can't see who's in the ceiling targeting us, but I can see the lasers once they discharge. I do my best to eyeball it and return fire. The other cadets move with confidence as they aim at our invisible targets. They aren't any more successful in downing our attackers than I am, but they certainly don't seem as confused. What do they know that I don't?

"Charlotte!" Rombag calls from beside me, "Turn on your infrared targeting!"

Infrared targeting? A shallow scowl pulls across my face. Of course the Izedis would be clued into that handy feature during their special armory training while the rest of us were left dead in the water.

"AI," I mumble into my helmet. "Activate infrared."

The cafeteria's sterile black and white interior instantly explodes into vibrant hues of yellow, red, blue, and green. The snap to thermal imaging burns my eyes, but I force myself not to shut them. Instead, I focus on the ceiling and see tall, orange figures flipping around the support beams.

There are only six Quinzentenians attacking us, but the group's size doesn't discount their destructive capabilities. They spin, twist, and swing through the air with the dexterity of acrobats as they rain fire down on me and the Izedis. They have the perfect balance of speed, agility, and accuracy, even while gliding between beams. As misplaced as my awe is, I can't help but be astonished by their movement. It's almost like they're flying.

Something that sounds like an Inovarian curse word rings out to my right. I look over in time to see Rombag rip off his helmet and throw it at a Quinzentenian in one swift motion. I would have gawked for a second longer if I didn't have to dodge the laser aimed at my chest.

"What're you doing?"

"Shoot!" Rombag commands as he does the same. I track his ammunition's energy signature until it connects with a Quinzentenian's calf. The force of impact pushes the soldier off of his perch. He lands on one of the tables with a loud *bang!* and a strangled groan. Rombag's smirk lets me know that wasn't a lucky shot. His brief display of confidence reassures me that he's in no more danger than the rest of us. If he can locate the cloaked Quinzentenians, surely he can avoid getting shot by them (right?).

I divert my thoughts from Rombag and focus solely on the Quinzentenians. With the infrared sensors on, my helmet automatically zeros in on the closest target for me, which is somewhat helpful, but this technology definitely doesn't make this firefight a stroll on the beach. Our overhead attackers are freakishly nimble, so it's tricky to keep them in the crosshairs for long.

My targeting system bounces around my screen like a ping pong ball. The flurry of movement strains my eyes to the point that I'm tempted to just close them. Despite my visual disorientation, I'm far from blind to the dangers at hand.

My abilities allow me to keep abreast of the treacherous trapeze artists. I can feel their weapons fire before my helmet's sensors alert me to the danger even when the charges are coming from behind. By the time my armor's AI tells me to move, I'm already out of the way.

Every time I pivot to return fire, I use my helmet to double-check my aim. By the time I do, my target's out of frame. I grit my teeth the fifth time this happens. If my body has a better and faster radar than the helmet does, why don't I just eyeball it?

"AI deactivate infrared," I command.

"Warning," the robotic voice replies. "Deactivation can result in—"

"Do it!"

The AI announces deactivation before my vision returns to normal. Without the sensory overload of the infrared targeting system, my head feels a lot clearer. With a deep breath, I allow my abilities to take control. My instincts drive my actions, telling me when and where to shoot. I find myself moving more fluidically.

Unfortunately, the same can't be said for the Izedis.

While they have much more experience training in armor than I do, the technology can only do so much for them in terms of dodging. My fellow humans dive, duck, and weave out of harm's way to the best of their abilities, but that's obviously not good enough. Combating an overhead enemy is extremely difficult under normal circumstances, but the Quinzentenians' acrobatic feats make it exponentially harder to land a shot. Inversely, we're easy pickings.

Several of the Izedis have been incapacitated. If it weren't for my mask, I'm sure I would have been overwhelmed by the scent of searing flesh. The Quinzentenians' lasers have cut holes through my comrades' armor, bodies, and bones, leaving the wounds cauterized.

I charge forward to shoot one of the Quinzentenians when one of the Izedi girls is knocked off her feet as her shoulder is blasted to bits. While I don't know her—or really anyone on this team, the sight of her exposed bone gives me chills. Whatever athletic aspirations she had before are totaled. I'm not sure if I'd even wish that on my worst enemy.

Her body is flung into mine so violently that the two of us are knocked to the floor in a heap of tangled limbs. I shove the girl off me in my rush to pay back the soldier who harmed her. Just like the enemy Rombag downed, my victim crashes to the floor like a comet. The man's cloak goes offline seconds after his fall. I can see him clutching his shoulder tightly. Looks like I shattered it the same way he shattered the Izedi girl's. How grimly ironic.

I muffle the remorse budding in my chest as the man's pain renders him unconscious. These people obviously enjoy hurting us, why should I have any qualms about returning the favor?

They started it, I remind myself.

I jump back from a foot shot.

I slide behind an overturned table to catch my breath. There's an unconscious Quinzentenian beside me. The sight of his charred flesh makes me gag. There's a hole in his side. My hand reaches out on its own. Should I? Is he even—?

I retract my hand. *No, remember,* **they** *started it.*

I take a deep breath that turns to a sniffle which ends in a splutter. *Oh my God, this too much. I—*

My thoughts stop short as my body prickles for a moment. I'm on my feet again. A laser burns where I was sitting seconds ago. I fire back and hear a screech from that direction. I keep a grip on the guilt.

They started it.

That attacker doesn't return fire, so I pick a new target and shoot again. This time I clip a woman out of midair. She's lucky enough to land on an equally unfortunate unconscious cadet. The teen's body softens her fall. The Quinzentenian clutches her chest tightly. I dry heave as I locate her wound. Had I been a few inches to the left, I would have hit her heart. Suddenly my chest feels tight, too.

They started it. They started it, they started it, they started it, they star—

Maybe I should put my infrared sensors back on.

"AI," I wheeze, "activ—*AH!*"

Several loud booms interrupt my command. I take cover behind one of the flipped-over tables. The room starts filling with smoke.

"Infrared!" I yell. The thermographic lens comes online with a flash. The smoke is light green through this filter, so it doesn't obstruct my view of the two orange figures escaping through the cafeteria doorway. I look up at the ceiling to search for anyone else in the rafters. Empty.

I leap to my feet to chase after them when a voice cuts through the air.

"Cadets, hold position!"

I stop in my tracks, as do the remaining cadets. Rombag has us stand at attention until the smoke clears. Once visibility returns to normal, I turn off my infrared and wait for instructions. Our commander orders half of the remaining Izedis to secure our incapacitated foes and bring them to the brig for interrogation.

My fellow cadets don't let Rombag's previously unseen face trip them up for more than a few moments. They quickly do as they're told. The commander and I were lucky enough—well, *I* was lucky. He just has skill—to land demobilizing shots on four of our six opponents, the other two escaping moments ago.

While they're busy securing prisoners, I tend to the downed Izedis. I can't do much for their laser burns, but I can use the bandages in my utility belt to slow the bleeding from the non-cauterized wounds. I do my best to keep my touch gentle. They're in enough pain as it is.

"You four," Rombag starts, pointing to the cadets tying up our captives. "Escort the Quinzentenians to the brig. Use your holo-watch for directions and stay alert. You made the mistake of letting your guard down once. Don't let it happen again."

Rombag turns to face the rest of us. "Those who are too injured or scared to be of use, fall back to the infirmary. The rest of you, follow me. The Pagi unit sent out a distress call when the attack started, and now they're unresponsive."

Besides me, only four other cadets take a step forward to fight beside him. My face sinks into a scowl. The Izedis were a group of fifteen battle-ready soldiers two hours ago. Now eight of them are too injured to fight and three are too paralyzed with fear to function, leaving four to fight God knows how many aliens. I stare at my retreating comrades as they limp through the doors, all eleven leaning on each other for strength in one way or another.

It's sick how much damage the Quinzentenians did in a matter of minutes.

My heart rate slowly inclines as heat crawls through my veins, my breath now quick and shallow. My disgust for the Quinzentenians flares and festers until the battle-borne pangs of guilt from earlier fizzle out. We've done absolutely nothing to these people, yet they invade our ship and cut us down without warning. It only took six of them to permanently ruin more than half of the Izedis' lives. I can only imagine how many of them are torturing the Pagis at the moment.

Adrenaline drums at my nerves at the thought of my team laying at the Quinzentenians' feet. I clutch my fists, the sensation both invigorating and nauseating. I need to stop these monsters before anyone else gets hurt.

Rombag is about to give the Izedis and me the "move out" order when I put my hand up to stop him. He pauses at my gesture.

I slide off my head gear and offer it to him.

"Take my helmet."

Surprise followed by confusion flashes across Rombag's features. For a while he just stares at the offering. My patience grows thin, so I shove the helmet into his chest.

"Take it," I repeat. "I don't need it. You know what I can do, and you've seen how quickly I react. If we're going to help the others, we need to be at our best, right? You need this to be at your prime, but I have enough adrenaline in my system to be good."

"Cadet, I cannot, in good conscience, take the armor of another sol—"

"Xiomoazi and the Pagis don't have time for this," I interject. "We can argue ethics *after* the Quinzentenians are in the brig."

My commanding officer, much to my surprise, lets out a light chuckle. "Now you're thinking like a soldier." He slips on the helmet, quickly readjusts the settings, and gives me a nod of appreciation. "Soldiers, move out!"

First-Person Secondary Character POV

———

I always joke that the first-person secondary character (FPSC) point of view is the Mom and Pop perspective since it's perfect for parental anecdotes. Whenever parents talk about their kids' childhoods, they typically use the FPSC POV because they're both observers and participants in those flashbacks. When they recount the highlights of their children's adolescence, they mostly comment on their mini-me's actions and reactions, only mentioning their involvement with each event as needed. An FPSC narrator operates the exact same way.

DEFINITION

Stories narrated from the first-person secondary character (FPSC) POV are told by a character that is not the protagonist. This speaker does not have direct access to the central character's thoughts, but for what they lack in detail, they make up for with commentary. FPSC narrators (FPSCNs) are often a member of the protagonist's entourage and know them well enough to make informed assessments of their actions.

It's important to note that the speaker's relationship with the hero makes their analyses inherently subjective. Just as it's impossible for anyone to have a truly objective opinion on literally anything, FPSCNs' past experiences and preferences dictate the manner with which they talk about the protagonist and how they interpret their actions. For instance, if an FPSCN adores the main character, their tone will reflect that affection; inversely, if they loathe the lead, the narration will speak to their hatred just as clearly.

While the FPSC narrator's main purpose is to follow the protagonist's journey, I'd like to take a second to reiterate that they are separate characters with their own thoughts, feelings, and backstory independent of (but relevant to) the central character. The FPSC POV removes readers from the conventional tunnel-visioned scope the first person operates within to show how the protagonist's actions affect others. The FPP POV uses observations and dialogue to determine other characters' reactions to the hero's decisions, but the FPSC POV lets readers know what secondary characters feel about the plot's progression. This insight speaks to the protagonist's personal growth and the function they serve within their community or society.

PERSPECTIVE HIGHLIGHTS

CULTURE

As informed narrators, FPSCNs know the protagonist well enough to provide audiences with a close read of the character's actions in relation to their personality and background. The FPSC POV is ideal for authors who want to explore the sociocultural aspects of fiction. This perspective allows writers to dive into their characters' backgrounds by analyzing the lead's choices in regard to their upbringing or heritage. When the narrator is a part of the protagonist's family, readers are able to understand how the protagonist's home life, region, culture, and religion influence how they conduct themselves.

These details also provide a contrast between how the narrator believes the protagonist should act and feel and what the character actually does. This tension often resonates with readers because many people understand how it feels to be conflicted between social norms, cultural and familial expectations, and their own desires. Take the following original short story, for example:

"A CHILD, FOR ONCE"

I've known Abidemi since we were six, but in all that time, she's never been a child.

Everyone knows that the first-born girl in an African household is typically treated like a second mother, but Abidemi had it worse than most. Her dad was diagnosed with cancer when we were eight, and her mom had to work two jobs to keep the family afloat. Unable to afford professional ones, Abidemi became her little siblings' babysitter *and* her father's caretaker. She was the woman of the house, tasked with cooking, cleaning, and caring for her one-year-old brother and two-year-old sister until her mom came home (which was, on average, no earlier than 10:00 p.m. and well past bedtime). Her Saturday mornings were free, though, because that's when her mom would take her dad to the doctor.

I remember how excited she used to be for her day off. She'd always skip going to her father's appointments, opting to use her leisure time away from her family. Every Saturday morning, rain or shine, Abidemi would meet me at my place a few doors down, and we'd play until her family came back home in the early afternoon.

Most of the time, we'd end up at the park and run around until our legs gave out. I *hated* the park—I was a lazy indoors kid with a grudge against exercise—but I'd spend the morning doing whatever Abidemi wanted to do, just to see her Saturday Smile, the grin reserved for her few hours of respite.

When we turned twelve, her Saturday Smile was hard to come by. Her father lost his fight with cancer that year, leaving behind thousands of dollars in medical expenses. Abidemi's mother had to take on more work to keep the vicious debt collectors at bay, so for the next six years, Abidemi was nothing but the nanny.

She forwent joining clubs, going to football games, dances, and parties, the whole nine yards to take care of her siblings. I helped when I could by babysitting the kids here and there to give her a chance to relax or made her skip class with me to see the forgotten Saturday Smile on a Tuesday. It was a risky move for two first-generation teens to make, but at the end of the day, the memories always made up for the sore bottoms.

Our most dull but important ditch day was spent filling out college applications. Abidemi wanted to cure cancer so it didn't ruin anyone else's childhood as it did hers, and I was going to make sure that she had the chance to try. I used the money from my part-time job to pay for her application fees, and it was worth every penny.

Abidemi and I both got into San Jose State University as microbiology and journalism majors respectively. We both cried when we got our acceptance letters, though for drastically different reasons. Mine were tears of joy, but Abidemi sobbed in distress. She knew she'd have to tell her mother that she was moving upstate.

Her mother's first words were "Who's going to help me raise these kids?" when Abidemi told her about SJSU.

"They weren't mine to raise in the first place!" was Abidemi's response.

Expectedly, she got a slipper thrown at her for the retort, and this became a recurring argument until the day she moved out. My friend cried in my passenger seat on and off from her driveway in San Diego until around Bakersfield. She'd never been away from home before. She'd miss the trio she left behind even if they ran her into the dirt.

She was silent from the tip of Bakersfield until Fresno. She started talking by the time we hit the San Luis Reservoir, but good Lord, after Gilroy, she was a giggly mess. Abidemi did nothing but laugh and sing for the whole home stretch to San Jose State. I'd seen that Saturday Smile more in those thirty minutes than I had in years.

"Nita, we're finally here!" Abidemi whooped as my car parked in front of our dorm. "I've been dreaming about this since we were eight!"

I watched my best friend skip toward the building. It was a very juvenile action from such a serious person. I couldn't help but grin at the sight. It seemed like college would give Abidemi the chance to be a child, for once.

ANALYSIS

In this original short story, my first-person secondary character, Nita, follows her best friend Abidemi as they grow up. As an FPSCN, Nita helps drive the story's plot, but her primary focus is to contextualize Abidemi's life story. She informs readers of the cultural, familial, and economic circumstances that lead our protagonist to live such a restricted life. Nita, as a first-generation child of immigrants herself, retains a sympathetic tone throughout her narration because she understands why Abidemi is so devoted to her family beyond pure obedience.

If I were to rewrite "A Child, For Once" in Abidemi's point of view, it would be a completely different piece even if it contains the same events. The short story would carry a much more solemn tone from the FPP POV simply because Abidemi shouldered a lot of responsibility from a young age. I'd reasonably linger on her primary goal, taking care of her family, rather than her mini adventures with her friend. Inversely, Nita's role is to help Abidemi enjoy life, so her narration reflects that mission by integrating positive memories and uplifting comments into the prose.

"A Child, For Once" being written from any other perspective, Abidemi's or otherwise, would change the central focus of the text and the overall feeling. No other narrator would be able to convey Nita's same fondness for her friend. A second or third-person narrator, as an impartial party, could explain our protagonist's plight to a certain degree, but the speaker's distance from the text wouldn't allow the affectionate undertone of "A Child, For Once" to speak for itself.

CHARACTER GROWTH

FPSC speakers are great for showing how a character has changed over time. The narrator's understanding of the protagonist's moral background allows them to provide predictions on what choices the protagonist is going to make. These projections can be accurate and further reinforce to the audience the consistency of the character's personality, or the narrator can be wrong, which shows the character's development.

For example, if the protagonist is a habitually selfish person, the narrator would expect them to save themselves in a life-or-death situation. When the protagonist puts another character's well-being first, the narrator's assessment of this unusual occurrence will show how much the character has changed over the course of the story. It would also highlight the fact that FPSC speakers, though knowledgeable, aren't omniscient.

The FPSC POV is the exciting middle ground between "You never really know someone" and "You know me better than I know myself." The FPSCN can predict some of the protagonist's actions, but they are subject to blindsiding plot twists as well. Writers can use these narrators to generate emotional reactions to unexpected events, especially when it comes to betrayal arcs.

This perspective allows authors to explore the speaker's hurt while the character tries to make sense of the protagonist's sudden change in behavior. As any normal person would, the FPSCN would take the treachery personally, so their feelings would likely taint their narration. This compromised position forces readers to dissect the prose to determine whether the speaker's perspective on the main character and plot's events is warped by their pain.

The first-person secondary character point of view was created to give commentary and insight into the protagonist's journey. It is an emotional, exciting, but extremely subjective perspective. Unlike a third-person narrator, an FPSCN will never be objective since people are inherently biased, as the following essay goes to show.

Moby Dick

Be it said, that though I had felt such a
strong repugnance . . . yet see how elastic
our stiff prejudices grow when love once
comes to bend them. For now I liked nothing better than to have Queequeg smoking
by me . . . because he seemed to be full of
such serene household joy then.

ISHMAEL IN *MOBY DICK* BY HERMAN MELVILLE

One of the most interesting instances of a first-person
secondary character (FPSC) narrator is found in Herman
Melville's world-famous classic *Moby Dick* (1851). Melville
shifts perspectives throughout his novel according to each
chapter's theme (*Moby Dick* is equal parts narrative and
whale philosophy, so he bounces around a lot), and it seems
that the FPSC POV was his favorite perspective to explore
friendships. In Chapters 3 and 10-12 ("The Spouter Inn,"

"A Bosom Friend," "Nightgown," and "Biographical"), Ishmael, the narrator, notes his impressions of Queequeg (the novel's shining star) as he gets to know the harpooner.

> No man prefers to sleep two in a bed. In fact, you would a good deal rather not sleep with your own brother . . . beget in me an uncomfortable feeling towards the man whom you design for my bedfellow . . .

> ". . . I take to be good evidence that this harpooneer is stark mad, and I've no idea of sleeping with a madman; and you, sir, *you* I mean, landlord, *you*, sir, by trying to induce me to do so knowingly, would thereby render yourself liable to a criminal prosecution."

To be blunt, Ishmael, a nineteenth-century New Englander, is a prejudiced person. He initially fears Queequeg because the man is his physical, ethnic, and religious opposite. Ishmael portrays the Rokovoko native as a murderous psychopath before ever meeting him. Melville masterfully leans into his narrator's baseless anxieties to build suspense in the moments before the pair's first encounter. Throughout this entire scene, you can palpably feel Ishmael's dread as he waits to meet the harpooner:

> I sat down on the side of the bed, and commenced thinking about this head-peddling harpooneer, and his door mat . . . I heard a heavy footfall in the passage, and saw a glimmer of light come into the room from under the door.

> Lord save me, thinks I, that must be the harpooneer, the infernal head-peddler. But

I lay perfectly still, and resolved not to say a word till spoken to. Holding a light in one hand, and that identical New Zealand head in the other, the stranger entered the room, and without looking towards the bed, placed his candle a good way off from me on the floor in one corner, and then began working away at the knotted cords of the large bag I before spoke of as being in the room . . . At first I knew not what to make of this; but soon an inkling of the truth occurred to me. I remembered a story of a white man—a whaleman too—who, falling among the cannibals, had been tattooed by them. I concluded that this harpooneer, in the course of his distant voyages, must have met with a similar adventure. And what is it, thought I, after all! It's only his outside; a man can be honest in any sort of skin. But then, what to make of his unearthly complexion . . .

This excerpt speaks to the unreliable nature of FPSC's. There is no guarantee that an FPSCN will be a kindhearted, socially aware, nondiscriminatory individual who views the protagonist through rose-colored lenses. Ishmael is apprehensive toward Queequeg for being born and raised differently than he was and narrates according to his feelings. Readers are only able to interact with the harpooner through this partisan perspective, which speaks to the power FPSCNs have on their audience. We only know what the narrator tells us, so there's no way around encountering their biases (though how we choose to interpret and critique those opinions is entirely our choice).

> I felt a melting in me. No more my splintered heart and maddened hand were turned against the wolfish world. This soothing savage had redeemed it. There he sat, his very indifference speaking a nature in which there lurked no civilized hypocrisies and bland deceits. Wild he was; a very sight of sights to see; yet I began to feel myself mysteriously drawn towards him. And those same things that would have repelled most others, they were the very magnets that thus drew me. I'll try a pagan friend, thought I . . . I drew my bench near him, and made some friendly signs and hints, doing my best to talk with him meanwhile.

Thankfully, Ishmael doesn't hold onto his (Queequeg-specific) xenophobia for long. After a happenstance bonding day full of keen observations and insightful conversations, the two are as thick as thieves. Ishmael's entire tone changes with this new development.

The previously fearful New Englander lavishes his new friend with compliments once he realizes that Queequeg is a good person. As mentioned earlier in this chapter, the FPSC POV is perfect for tracking how the protagonist has changed in the eyes of their peers. Melville could have used the third-person omniscient perspective to note how Ishmael's opinions shift, but he would have fallen short of embodying the sincerity of Ishmael's newfound affection and weighing remorse over his misconceptions. Take the following lines, for example:

> With much interest I sat watching him. Savage though he was, and hideously marred about the face—at least to my taste—his countenance

yet had a something in it which was by no means disagreeable. You cannot hide the soul. Through all his unearthly tattooings, I thought I saw the traces of a simple honest heart; and in his large, deep eyes, fiery black and bold, there seemed tokens of a spirit that would dare a thousand devils. And besides all this, there was a certain lofty bearing about the Pagan, which even his uncouthness could not altogether maim.

A third-person omniscient narrator would be able to tell you that Ishmael's observations led him to change his mind, but this first-person account carries an undertone of love that *shows* the extent of his character growth and errors. The contrast between how Queequeg was initially and is currently described adds layers to him as well. Melville uses the FPSC POV to speak to the unwarranted hatred the darling character faces, showing readers how prejudice can warp people's perceptions.

Queequeg is a consistently kind, doting, and generous character throughout the entire novel, yet Ishmael's distorted view gives the harpooner a redemption arc because the speaker had to work through his own biases. This FPSC narration style further endears readers to this protagonist because his once villainous image is now near angelic.

He seemed to take to me quite as naturally and unbiddenly as I to him; and when our smoke was over, he pressed his forehead against mine . . . in his country's phrase, that we were bosom friends; he would gladly die for me, if need should be. In a countryman, this sudden flame of friendship would have seemed far too premature, a thing to be much distrusted; but in this simple savage those old rules would not apply.

This is my absolute favorite quote from *Moby Dick*. Every time I reread this passage, Ishmael's warmhearted words make me feel an influx of affection for Queequeg and brings to mind my fond memories surrounding this scene. I first read "A Bosom Friend" during my senior year at Georgia State University. My American Romanticism class was supposed to cover at least ten chapters of *Moby Dick* during the seventy-five-minute period, but we only got three done because we spent the majority of the time gushing over this chapter's tone.

We all agreed that Ishmael's fondness was tangible because his words spoke to the beauty, excitement, and buzz behind their budding friendship. The lecture went at least twenty minutes over time because our group was so enamored by Queequeg that we forgot that we had other places to be. For the rest of that semester, our conversations would continuously derail back to this passage because it's such a remarkable feat of character development. To date, the handful of us that are still in contact continue to call each other "bosom friend" in homage to our favorite friendship arc.

The first-person secondary character point of view is such a phenomenal perspective because it allows us to see how much the narrator's personal feelings can affect how the protagonist is portrayed. "Bosom Friend," one of the most famous chapters of Melville's *Moby Dick*, is a prime example of how the narrator's perception of the lead dictates the reading experience. As Ishmael overcame his prejudices,

Queequeg, the chapter's protagonist, shifted from a frightening "savage" to an endearing character worthy of Ishmael's (and our!) affections.

Incipience First-Person Secondary Character

———

The more time you spend with a person, the more you get to know them. You pick up on what they like, love, hate, and outright despise through observations and conversations. After a while, these interactions allow you to ascertain shifts in their moods and mindsets with little to no verbal communication. Rombag, Mali's commanding officer, has spent hours arguing with the protagonist over the morality and necessities of war, so he has the necessary insight to serve as her narrator.

Throughout *Incipience*, he insists that her perspective on conflict will change after her first battle, and she argues just the opposite. Once the Quinzentenians ambush their team, her sense of self-preservation takes over, and she reflexively does quite a bit of damage. As her first-person secondary narrator, Rombag compares Mali's initial resolve to her actions to show readers just how quickly she's willing to compromise her pacifistic beliefs to save her teammates.

ROMBAG

I signal for the cadets to halt. We've combed through the entire route but haven't seen a single Quinzentenian. If the other teams had encountered them, they would have requested backup by now. I glance down at my holo-watch. The blank screen is devoid of any missed alerts, which should be a good sign, but my experience with these people lets me know that it's anything but.

I order the cadets to secure the perimeter. They do so silently and hold their positions as instructed. Fifteen minutes pass before the group reminds me of a critical fact: patience is *not* a human virtue. Now that the earlier adrenaline has waned, tension bleeds from the young adults' posture. I snarl at the sight. Dead soldiers are typically inattentive ones first. Even if there is no one in the room now, we can't let our guard down.

I open my mouth to tell the Izedis to focus when one catches my eye. While the rest have grown lax, this recruit stands at attention. Even though the humans look identical with their matching all-black armor and opaque helmets, I can identify Cadet Charlotte-Amalie Joseph by her posture.

Every so often, she shifts her footing to avoid stiffness, as runners tend to do, but she's otherwise standing at attention. Her blaster remains firmly in hand, and her finger hovers over the trigger. She's battle-ready even though she doesn't want to be.

It's a reassuring sight—at least someone else is taking this seriously—but an odd one. Cadet Joseph has been adamantly against fighting from her first day of training, so I half-expected her to slip away during our march here. Yet here she is: armed, vigilant, and primed for action.

There is a brief pause in her movements. Her shoulder slumps for a moment, and she shakes her head. I suspect the gesture was paired with her infamous "side-eye," as she calls it. The human has as low tolerance for incompetence as I do—one of our few commonalities—so the Izedis' lackadaisical attitude has likely struck a nerve.

Cadet Joseph breaks from her position against the wall to approach me. Her strides are quick and stiff, a far cry from her usual stroll. Something's amiss beyond the obvious. She only looks that tense before someone attacks her.

"Commander," she starts. "Something isn't right. I think we should g—"

She rushes forward to tackle me, her arms wrapping around my midsection the second before my world begins to tilt backward. My helmet surges with concentrated heat. My ears ring as my visor wrinkles, ripples, and shatters before my eyes. My nose burns as my protectant's inner circuitry crackles, and my tongue smarts as the sparks catch my mouth. My body cuts through the air, numb for the seconds before my back slams against the cool tile. Cadet Joseph lands on my chest, her helmet hammering the air out of my lungs.

I give an undignified wheeze while she, much to her credit, is unfazed by the fall. She's on her feet returning fire in an instant. I try to sit up to help fend off the ambush, but my head is still reeling. Cadet Joseph's image is doubled, and my ears hear nothing but white noise. I stay still until there's only one of her and the ringing stops.

By the time I can see well enough to stand, she's at my side. She pulls me up the rest of the way. Her helmet's voice modulator makes her words monotonous as intended, but her rapid-fire speech hints at her anxiety.

"Commander, are you okay?"

I give her a short nod before unholstering my blaster and activating my infrared sensors. Cadet Joseph's hand twitches like she wants to reach out but jumps back to avoid being shot before she can. That's all it takes to get her back on track. The cadet dodges attacks flawlessly, but her return fire seems slower than usual. Ironically, the proclaimed pacifist shoots exceptionally well, so there's no reason for her to miss as many targets as she has, especially the Quinzentenian standing right above us. What is she, blind?

Wait . . . she is.

"Joseph!" I call.

An Izedi with the same name turns at the sound of my voice. "Yes, sir?"

"Not you!" I reply. He barely avoids getting shot in his moment of distraction.

"Charlotte," I yell, opting for her first name to spare the boy any further disruptions. "Turn on your infrared sensors!"

She nods, and within seconds, her movements become more confident. Her infrared is an aid, but mine is currently a hindrance. My sensors shift in and out of focus as they try to compensate for the shattered circuit boards. I let out a loud string of curses. My helmet is too damaged to function.

I quickly holster my blaster, rip off the cracked helmet and throw it in the direction that Cadet Joseph is shooting.

"What're you *doing?*" She screeches.

I respond to her question with a command. "Shoot!"

I see her pause in my peripheral, but my focus is on the Quinzentenian standing on the pillar right in front of me. Their invisibility cloak ripples the air around them, so I shoot a few inches from the edge. The force of impact pushes the soldier off his perch. He crashes onto a table with a loud *bang!* and a strangled groan. I smirk. *This is why I train cadets without gadgets!*

Cadet Joseph springs into action the moment my target is floored. It's a shame that she'd been resistant to being a soldier prior to this point. She is an irrefutably excellent fighter and a competent marksman. If she were to fully commit to the military, she would climb the ranks just as quickly as I did. Given her regenerative healing capabilities, she'd likely progress faster, if anything.

The thought's as perfect as it is implausible. The teen retches forward every time she hits her mark, evidentially nauseous at the sight of burnt and bleeding wounds. She looks like she's about to keel over by the time one of the Quinzentenians throws down a smoke bomb.

The gas quickly spreads. I can see Cadet Joseph pivot to give chase. I call out for her to hold position. The Quinzentenians are too weak to retaliate at the moment, and the downed cadets need medical attention. I'll handle them once my subordinates are attended to.

The Izedis and I stand at attention for several minutes before I order them to secure the Quinzentenians we incapacitated. No one made a kill shot, but Cadet Joseph certainly came close. One of her marks has a hole in their chest. Had the blow been a few inches to the left, it would've been fatal. As much as the Quinzentenians deserve it, I'm glad they all survived. I don't think the humans are ready for that moral dilemma just yet.

Besides, captives are more useful informants than corpses.

Cadet Joseph scurries past the Quinzentenian she shot and crouches down before Reese, the nearest wounded Izedi. She checks the young man's pulse with a slow and a seemingly soft touch. As a Pagi, she rarely interacts with my charges and has few reasons to dote over them. These people are essentially strangers, but she treats them with such tender care. She surprises me.

I divert my attention away from the two and check my holo-watch. The Pagis sent out a distress call once our firefight started, and now they're not responding.

"You four," I start, pointing to ones tying up our captives. "Escort the Quinzentenians to the brig. Use your holo-watch for directions and stay alert. You made the mistake of letting your guard down once. Don't let it happen again."

I address the remaining group. "Those who are too injured or scared to be of use, fall back to the infirmary. The rest of you, follow me. The Pagi unit sent out a distress call when the attack started, and now they're unresponsive."

Cadet Joseph immediately takes a step forward first, followed by four other cadets. There are more left who can fight, but they're too shaky to shoot straight. Our numbers aren't favorable, but at least we've minimized liabilities.

"Cadets mo—"

Cadet Joseph holds out her hand to silence me. She unclips her headgear and hands it to me.

"Take my helmet."

Her expression tells me that it's a command, not an offering. Cadet Joseph's head is held high, and her jaw is clenched tightly. The teen's seething brown eyes look black in the mess hall's flickering lights.

She would deny it until her dying breath, but she's a soldier at heart. Like Inovarian troops, she was raised to defend her people at all costs. Now that she knows that her *real* team, the Pagis, has been attacked, she seems ready and willing to reciprocate harm to ensure their safety.

"Take it," she repeats. "I don't need it. You know what I can do, and you've seen how quickly I react. If we're going to help the others, we need to be at our best, right? You need this to be at your prime, but I have enough adrenaline in my system to be good."

I try to hand the helmet back. As much as I appreciate the unexpected gesture, I can't leave her exposed. Her regenerative abilities are astonishing, but there's no guarantee she'd be able to survive a head shot.

"Cadet, I cannot, in good conscience, take the armor of another sol— "

"Xiomoazi and the Pagis don't have time for this," she interjects. "We can argue ethics *after* the Quinzentenians are in the brig."

I pause. After all the hours I've spent debating war ethics and policies with this human, she tells *me* to reevaluate my priorities? I can't help but let out a short laugh. I grab the helmet with a grateful nod.

"Now you're thinking like a soldier."

HOW THE STORY HAS CHANGED

Mali is a self-proclaimed pacifist who doesn't mind a fist-fight. In the first chapters of *Incipience,* she is strictly against warfare and bucks Rombag's military propaganda at every turn. She maintains this resolve until the Quinzentenians attack. Her pacifism is instantly sidelined as her will to survive asserts itself. She primarily focuses on her team's survival rather than the implications of her actions. Sure, she's empathetic to the Quinzentenians' pain and a little squeamish when it comes to blood, but she doesn't pause to note her ideological shift.

Her commander, however, takes note of her changed mindset and comments accordingly. As her FPSC narrator, Rombag compares Mali's advertised beliefs to her immediate actions. For all her rebuffs against the army, she makes the perfect soldier. She's attentive, follows orders, fights exceptionally well, cares for her comrades, and is brave to boot. Mali views herself as a survivor and begrudging participant, while Rombag sees her for what she is: a reluctant hero.

The Inovarian does more than identify Mali's inconsistencies; he highlights her positive attributes. The duo has a contentious relationship at best, so Rombag's compliments speak to Mali's character since the commendation was well earned (from an ordinarily reluctant source). The commander initially views our protagonist as a relatively selfish person because of her pacifistic stance, thinking she's unwilling to do her share in ending the war.

After observing Mali's reaction to the Izedis' defeat, he realizes that while she's opposed to killing, she is willing to do what it takes to protect those in her care. From that moment forward, he views her actions in a new light, especially as she tends to the wounded and sacrifices her helmet for him. Mali's a team player; she just needed to have hers endangered to act like it.

First-person secondary character narrators are perfect for giving us a close read on the protagonist's development. Just as Rombag highlights Mali's new attitude, other FPSC orators track changes in the main character's behavior. Lest they're a particularly introspective individual or going for a total rebrand, it's rare for a hero to note and deconstruct non-pivotal shifts in their personality.

Mali isn't inclined to ponder over the implications of her proactive attitude toward the end of this excerpt because she has more pressing issues in mind, and she quite frankly can't identify her newfound offensiveness as readily as Rombag does. Similarly, just as she's making subconscious changes, other FPPNs might not even notice their development until faced with an individual or obstacle that highlights their progression (or regression, depending on the plot). FPSCNs like Rombag proactively chart the protagonist's shifting mindsets throughout the plot to provide readers with detailed assessments of the character's behavior that we wouldn't otherwise receive.

First-Person Unreliable Narrator POV

From a young age, we are taught to evaluate the reliability of other people's statements. As children, our parents told us not to talk to strangers because they'd mislead us. As teenagers, we learned to differentiate between malicious rumors and well-meant warnings. As adults, we think twice before trusting just anyone with our personal information.

It's second nature to contemplate the validity of other people's words in real life, but we tend to take literary narration at face value. Some readers assume that the speaker has no motivation to skew information because they're fictional. There's no need to misrepresent what's not real, right?

Wrong. And here's why.

DEFINITION

Stories narrated in the first-person unreliable narrator (FPU) point of view are told by individuals whose words cannot be blindly accepted. These speakers' words are (often purposefully) disorienting and misleading because they carry double meanings. Throughout stories of this sort, authors drop hints that suggest that the narrator's credibility is somehow compromised. Once it is established that the narrator is unreliable, readers are meant to question and cross-examine every detail the speaker provides them.

PERSPECTIVE ATTRIBUTES

DISORIENTATION

Authors often use unreliable narrators to disorient their audience. They write with ambiguous language, contradicting statements, and/or omit information such as sensory details and vital plot information to achieve this effect. These exclusions force readers to question what the author's aim is and why they chose to be coy about their intentions. Texts with unreliable narrators are meant to generate conversation, especially when they include an unsolvable mystery. One heavily debated work of this sort is "Recitatif" (1983) by Toni Morrison.

In this phenomenal short story, Morrison is purposefully vague about her protagonist's demographic. "Recitatif" follows a girl named Twyla as she and her childhood best friend, Roberta, grow up and lead very different lives. The other kids at the orphanage saw them as an odd pair because they were an interracial duo in the 1950s. Readers learn that one of the girls is Black while one is White, but which child is which is purposefully omitted. To date, scholars and casual readers alike futilely debate the girls' demographics with no success. Morrison masterfully leaves us ignorant to their races to show that the story's themes of family, friendship, and strife are universally experienced (Morrison, 2007).

Writers who use speakers of this sort do well to take notes from the execution of "Recitatif." Morrison balanced omission, tension, and emotion to make her arguments about race relations. Had she written this work with a reliable narrator, the story would not have been as powerful. A straightforward narration would have stripped the text of its global message and impact, so it was fundamentally necessary for Morison to use an unreliable narrator. Writers always have to consider what they want their readers to know, but it's especially important in this perspective. The tension and conversations generated by this point of view are completely lost when authors fail to carefully consider how it influences their argument's impact and reception.

SOCIAL AWARENESS

Some narrators are forthcoming with their knowledge but are still considered unreliable because they have a skewed grasp of reality. They perceive events differently than they actually occur but retain the ability to notice some discrepancies between their perception and reality. This kind of narrator is most often, but not exclusively, a neurodivergent individual (someone who has a mental illness and/or is on the autistic spectrum) whose condition prevents them from understanding the world as other characters do. Some authors use such figures to draw attention to the ways individuals can interpret reality. For example, they may narrate a character comparing their warped self-image to what they actually look like to highlight the harsh realities of body dysmorphia.

This perspective can be just as puzzling as it is sobering. Unreliable narrators are perfect for psychological thrillers because they challenge readers to actively differentiate fact from fiction. The speaker's words cannot be taken at face value, so it's disorienting to decipher when their internal discourse is accurate, who they can trust, who's really there (i.e., Is Mrs. Jones real, or is she the narrator's comfort character?), and details of the sort. While crafting these intricate characters can be hard work, many authors find it worth the effort due to the level of reader engagement.

Beyond their educational value and thrill factor, unreliable narrators are avenues in which one can explore social arguments. My favorite thing about literature is that it teaches unknowledgeable and/or unaffected parties about the plights of those unlike them. Neurotypical, or "normal," individuals, by definition, have not experienced being neurodivergent. Reading a story narrated by an unreliable figure would educate readers on experiences and the politics surrounding them. The short story "The Yellow Wallpaper" (1892) by Charlotte Perkins Gilman is a perfect example of this.

> John laughs at me, of course, but one expects that in marriage.

> John is practical in the extreme. He has no patience with faith, an intense horror of superstition, and he scoffs openly at any talk of things not to be felt and seen and put down in figures.

> John is a physician, and *perhaps*—(I would not say it to a living soul, of course, but this is dead paper and a great relief to my mind)—*perhaps* that is one reason I do not get well faster.

> You see, he does not believe I am sick!

> And what can one do?

If a physician of high standing, and one's own husband, assures friends and relatives that there is really nothing the matter with one but temporary nervous depression—a slight hysterical tendency—what is one to do?

My brother is also a physician, and also of high standing, and he says the same thing.

So I take phosphates or phosphites—whichever it is, and tonics, and journeys, and air, and exercise, and am absolutely forbidden to "work" until I am well again.

Personally, I disagree with their ideas.

Personally, I believe that congenial work, with excitement and change, would do me good.

But what is one to do?

Gilman's story exemplifies what it was like to be a neurodivergent woman during the nineteenth century by highlighting how poor the health care was. "The Yellow Wallpaper" follows a woman who is isolated in her room to treat the "temporary nervous depression—a slight hysterical tendency" (which the text implies is actually postpartum depression) her physician husband diagnosed her with.

After prolonged seclusion, she slowly begins to see a person in her yellow wallpaper. She grows increasingly obsessed with the figure and goes as far as mauling the walls to get to the phantom. Her fixation on the wallpaper only spirals out of control because her caretakers believe that keeping her isolated with nothing but her thoughts is the best cure.

This treatment is faulty on all accounts, especially when we take into consideration that the wallpaper was assumably just as physically detrimental to the narrator as it was psychologically.

The decor likely contributed to her hallucinations since arsenic, a metalloid poison, was used to create yellow dyes in the late 1800s. The narrator literally clawed apart her room with her bare hands, so the toxins undoubtedly entered her body through her tattered nails or via direct inhalation as she chipped away at the wallpaper (Rae, 2016). The narrator's psychological breakdown was arguably preventable because had she been allowed to leave her room and interact with others, she would have never gotten the chance to saturate her system with the arsenic that likely led to her demise.

When I first read this story, I remember being shocked, appalled, and saddened that people who suffered from depression were treated in such a way in earlier centuries. At that time, I did not know much about mental health treatment (past or present), but Gilman's work opened my eyes to issues that didn't directly affect me and made me want to learn more about modern practices. Her unreliable narrator exposed forms of abuse that I was previously unaware of and deepened my understanding of the neurodivergent experience.

Had Gilman used another perspective, the emotional resonance of "The Yellow Wallpaper" would have fallen short. The narrator's first-person account embodies her deterioration through her thoughts and heightened agitation. Readers can feel her increasing urgency to free both herself and the woman from her wall through her change in tone. Any other perspective would not have been able to communicate her distress as well because the narrator would have been an observer with their own interpretations of her thoughts or an objective third party looking in.

The best way to learn about a person is to listen to their heartfelt expressions and try to put yourself in their position. Authors who write in the first-person unreliable narrator POV do well to explain neurodivergent experiences and empathize readers to the plights of others.

"The Tell-Tale Heart"

———

Edgar Allan Poe is *the* Gothic king of chaos. His short stories are full of creepy characters, haunting prose, and unreliable narrators that keep readers on the edge of their seats. Of Poe's plentiful lineup of dubious narrators, the protagonist of "The Tell-Tale Heart" (1843) takes the cake when it comes to being capricious.

The human mind has always been a fascinating topic, but it was especially enthralling to the general public during the nineteenth century. At that time, scholars delved into pseudo-sciences in efforts to explain the phenomena that is the human psyche. Poe took advantage of the buzz around psychology and wrote neurodivergent characters like the speaker of "The Tell-Tale Heart." He captured the attention of his contemporary and modern readers alike with the opening lines of the work:

> True!—nervous—very, very dreadfully nervous I had been and am; but why will you say that I am mad? The disease had sharpened my senses—not destroyed—not dulled them. Above all was the sense of hearing acute. I

heard all things in the heaven and in the earth.
I heard many things in hell. How, then, am I
mad? Hearken! and observe how healthily—
how calmly I can tell you the whole story.

This opening paragraph immediately sets the short story's tone. The narrator identifies his own mad reputation, compromised senses, and warped perception of reality all at once, showing readers why we cannot fully trust him. Poe makes the speaker argue with himself in an energetic and sporadic manner that further establishes his unreliable nature. This introduction contextualizes the rest of the story's contents and explains the protagonist's faulty logic.

It is impossible to say how first the idea entered
my brain; but once conceived, it haunted me
day and night. Object there was none. Passion
there was none. I loved the old man. He had
never wronged me. He had never given me
insult. For his gold I had no desire. I think it
was his eye! yes, it was this! He had the eye of
a vulture—a pale blue eye, with a film over it.
Whenever it fell upon me, my blood ran cold;
and so by degrees—very gradually—I made up
my mind to take the life of the old man, and
thus rid myself of the eye forever.

Now this is the point. You fancy me mad. Mad-
men know nothing. But you should have seen
me. You should have seen how wisely I pro-
ceeded—with what caution—with what fore-
sight—with what dissimulation I went to work!
I was never kinder to the old man than during
the whole week before I killed him.

If "The Tell-Tale Heart" were narrated by a neurotypical protagonist, the short story would have had a drastically different tone for a number of reasons. Readers would first and foremost be confused as to why someone in full control of their mental faculties would decide to kill their unsuspecting elderly roommate who had never wronged them. Most people would simply avoid the old man or move out altogether if his eye disturbed them that profusely, so murder would be a completely nonsensical resolution. Poe's protagonist, on the other hand, hyperfixates on these details to the point that his sense of logic completely escapes him.

His plotting is a by-product of his deep-seated obsession rather than actual feelings of hatred. He even admits that he loves the elderly fellow, a statement that stirs a sense of ambivalence in readers. His compromised mindset drives us to be concerned for both the perpetrator and the victim.

The first time I read "Tell-Tale Heart," I was distressed over the old man's impending doom, but I was sympathetic to the protagonist's plight because I realized that his roommate's unsightly eye fueled the narrator's descent to stark madness. My feelings about his actions volleyed between condemnation and concern because the speaker's misdeeds, as calculated as they are, are not rooted in any malice. Poe's protagonist is hard to hate because I understand why he acts as he does, even if I can't excuse it.

Authors who are interested in writing ignominious yet redeemable characters ought to wield unreliable narrators just as Poe did. These speakers are perfect for exploring the causation and morality of otherwise demented acts because they don't romanticize the character's sins. They, instead, make readers identify the warped (and at times tortured) mindsets that lead to egregious crimes. Poe's work doesn't glorify homicide by any means, but it does explain how an otherwise loving person can be driven to violence. Take the following passage, for example:

> Presently I heard a slight groan, and I knew it was the groan of mortal terror. It was not a groan of pain or of grief—oh, no!—it was the low stifled sound that arises from the bottom of the soul when overcharged with awe. I knew the sound well. Many a night, just at midnight, when all the world slept, it has welled up from my own bosom, deepening, with its dreadful echo, the terrors that distracted me. I say I knew it well. I knew what the old man felt, and pitied him, although I chuckled at heart.

To date, I have mixed feelings about Poe's protagonist because he's so unlike any other fictional criminal that I've encountered. His actions are by every definition atrocious, but they're not rooted in any form of maliciousness. He shows compassion for and sympathizes with his victim throughout the entire work, two feelings that directly contradict his actions. I can't help but feel for the two characters since both are afflicted by a terror that is out of their control.

Unstable narrators of this sort are unique in their ability to be both the hero and the villain. Just as the speaker is a victim of his own mind, authors can pen characters that are dangerous to themselves and others. While most people have a self-destructive habit or two that compromises their livelihood (deflection, projection, and my personal favorite, procrastination, just to name a few), unreliable narrators typically take ruinous actions to the next level.

I paced the floor to and fro with heavy strides, as if excited to fury by the observations of the men—but the noise steadily increased. Oh God! what could I do? I foamed—I raved—I swore! I swung the chair upon which I had been sitting, and grated it upon the boards, but the noise arose over all and continually increased. It grew louder—louder—louder! And still the men chatted pleasantly, and smiled. Was it possible they heard not? Almighty God!—no, no! They heard!—they suspected!—they knew!—they were making a mockery of my horror!—this I thought, and this I think. But anything was better than this agony! Anything was more tolerable than this derision! I could bear those hypocritical smiles no longer! I felt that I must scream or die! and now—again!—hark! louder! louder! louder! louder!

"Villains!" I shrieked, "dissemble no more! I admit the deed!—tear up the planks!—here, here!—It is the beating of his hideous heart!"

If Poe had chosen any other kind of narrator, this scene would have been outright perplexing. In most works, the moment the protagonist gets away with their crime, they feel smug, gratified, and euphoric even. The protagonist evidently didn't get that memo because he grew indignant once he realized that there was the slightest chance his misdeed would go undiscovered.

The average person would be inclined to celebrate (quite literally) getting away with murder and fly under the radar thereafter to ensure their nefarious deeds remain buried.

Poe's narrator, on the other hand, acts as the Scooby-Doo antithesis by impulsively revealing himself as a killer. This turn of events is consistent with the character's spastic behavior, yet readers are still awed. We can't fathom anyone in any mental condition sabotaging themselves to this extent.

The execution and reception of "Tell-Tale Heart" are fundamentally dependent on the narrator's unreliable nature. Had Poe written his character in any other perspective, the protagonist's motive, obsession, and confession would have been outright illogical, causing the work to fall short of the morally ambiguous masterpiece that it is.

Incipience First-Person Unreliable Narrator

———

Modern warfare is chaotic, but it's not lawless. There are sanctions on what kind of weapons nations can use, the areas they're allowed to fly over, and who they can attack to mitigate long-term and irrecoverable harm to a region. Whether institutions adhere to these rules is a completely different conversation, but the fact of the matter is they exist, and there are stipulations in place if a country breaks them.

This is how Earth's conflicts are regulated, but who's to say the same rules exist in space? The Inovarians and Quinzentenians have been fighting for six generations, and in that time, countless soldiers and civilians on both sides have fallen victim to a variety of attacks that we would consider war crimes. Quinzentenian Commander Unrok, a soldier of many years, is one of the many survivors who has been traumatized beyond belief and has had his psyche warped as a result of such tragedies.

COMMANDER UNROK

It's almost funny how vulnerable these people are, the humans and Inovarians alike. Despite their merciless training, they'll never accomplish much. Our rivals invest in their firepower and physical strength instead of their strategic skills, and that is why the war is ours to win.

For years, we have pushed our boundaries to invent stealth technologies to safeguard our soldiers and turn the tide in our favor. Our teleportation devices, for example, are far beyond what the Inovarians are capable of at the moment, as are our invisibility cloaks. My trainees and I have been sitting in these rafters for fifteen minutes now, unbeknownst to our hosts. The humans and Inovarians scuttle about their daily lives in the (poorly catered) cafeteria below, completely at our mercy and clueless to that fact.

I raise my blaster and aim at a few targets. I don't shoot, but it's satisfying to know that I can. I don't miss, you know. I could have killed them all already if I really wanted to. I won't, though. Captain Minókyt gave us strict orders to remain hidden unless we need another distraction. And so here my troops and I sit. Lying. Ready. Waiting.

A voice in my ear shakes me from my thoughts. My finger's closing in on the trigger by the time I register that it's Captain Minókyt speaking over our com system. Her voice is ordinarily soothing, but any unanticipated noise is startling to any real soldier.

"Vessel to away teams, the decoy units are going to set the alarms off in fifteen seconds. Brace yourselves, remember your missions, and Pekema Ima be with you in 5 . . . 4 . . . 3 . . . 2 . . .1 . . ."

*"A security breach has been detected. This is **not** a drill. All officers and cadets report to their stations immediately. This is **not** a drill. I repeat . . ."*

I cover my ears to mute the sound, the sirens clawing away at them. The sound itself isn't unbearable, but the memories associated with it are. Flashes of boarding parties gone wrong run through my head. I try to stave off the images of dead comrades and bloodied corridors to no avail. As usual, my psyche is not cooperative. The scenes run their course until the alarm cuts off.

I lean back on a support beam to catch my breath, grateful for the privacy my cloak grants. No soldier should see their commanding officer panicking during a mission.

By the time I regain my composure, the humans are long gone. The cafeteria is more intriguing now that it's empty. The Earthlings abandoned everything. Untouched and half-eaten plates lay deserted, and several fear-induced spills litter the floor. A few of the trash cans are knocked over, likely toppled by those blinded by fear.

It's clear that these soldiers aren't as battle-hardened as the Inovarians, though that's not much of a surprise, given their youth. The Inovarians start training their soldiers at younger ages than we (and apparently humans) do, so they're likely inexperienced and scared. My soldiers are just as green, but they're disproportionately calm.

As I sit here watching my subordinates, it's clear that they don't understand the severity of our situation. All five are at ease now that the humans are gone. They know that we won't get to fight unless one of the teams calls for backup, an unlikely event given the soldiers selected for this mission. The captain only wanted the best, but I convinced her to let my trainees participate to get some experience. She said they could come if I supervise them and make sure they stay out of the way. The six of us are fail-safes at best, but that doesn't mean they shouldn't take their jobs seriously.

Four of my five soldiers talk among themselves to pass the time while the fifth, First Recruit Poním, entertains himself more recklessly. The young man lazily tosses his blaster through the air and catches it to keep himself occupied. He feels my eyes on him and looks my way mid-catch. That split attention allows his blaster to slip past his fingers. He barely manages to grab it before it falls past his reach, though his blind snatch comes with a consequence. One of his fingers catches the trigger, accidentally shooting a trashcan. I swing over to his rafter and swat the back of his head.

"Don't blow our cover, you idiot!"

He gives a genuine apology, and I hit him one more time for good measure before returning to my post.

These children are painfully lackadaisical about this mission despite my warnings. They're too inexperienced to know that fear and vigilance keep soldiers alive. Pekema Ima forbid, they may die before they learn that lesson. The Inovarians are not to be underestimated. That much I know.

These damned youths haven't seen a real battle before. Sure, they've gotten their hands dirty with minor skirmishes, but they haven't seen the Inovarians' real tactics. We stopped fighting army-to-army on the battlefield nearly thirty years ago, so these kids haven't seen anything up close and personal. They wouldn't be so calm if they had seen what I have, known what I know.

They'd be rightfully scared if they'd taken the time to stop and listen to my stories. I tried to warn them about what those people can do. How cruel they can be. They enjoy killing Quinzentenians, seeing us writhe. I'm sure they prefer psychological pain as opposed to physical. We heal quickly, and our doctors can mend just about anything short of death, but they can only do so much for our heads. The Inovarians know that, so they've found ways to compromise our minds.

I remember when the king and queen stopped sending us to Inova to fight. We were winning a skirmish by a landslide until their ship passed overhead and showered us with this green substance. We laughed at first, thinking that the sticky gel was some sort of glue to slow us down, but that was before it seeped into our skin.

The poison clawed its way through our veins, making us feel as if we were freezing from the inside out. Once the initial chills subsided, the hallucinations began. The world warped in front of our eyes in sporadic bursts, making us see things and people who weren't even there. Many of us mistook our brothers in arms for our enemies during that haze. The majority of Quinzentenian deaths that day were not at the hands of Inovarians.

I am among the handful who were lucky to leave the planet alive and well. The memories of that fatal day still haunt me, but I've otherwise lived a fine life—retired early, trained two generations of damn good soldiers. I turned out better than most. To date, many of the other unlucky souls I was deployed with still suffer from those intense chills and hallucinations.

The sound of boots clattering on the floor interrupts my musings. My soldiers perk up at the sound and silently prime themselves for action as the sound grows louder.

Good. They're not completely senseless.

I direct my attention to the cafeteria door as the sound grows nearer. A tall, black-clad figure marches into the room followed by smaller, similarly dressed ones. He stands tall and proud in the middle of the room while the others fan out to secure it. No real use since we're up here, but I'm gracious enough to acknowledge a good effort when I see it.

I change my glasses from infrared to binocular mode to get a better look at the man standing in the middle of the room. I can tell he's the only Inovarian here. His armor looks more worn than the others, and it's well embellished. He has a dozen or so pins and patches on his uniform, while the humans have none.

I clench my jaw at the sight of him. I'm sure the only way to earn that level of decoration is by doing something monumental. He was probably there when his fellow monsters poisoned us. Of course he was. The foot soldiers that day had just as many patches.

I can picture him now: his black gloves painted red with our blood and embellished with our entrails as he took the time to disembowel each of his victims with the knife on his belt. His robotic cackling and my comrades' cries reverb through my ears. My hands itch to wrap around his throat and squeeze until he chokes on his laughter.

Oh, what I'd give for the chance to feel him go limp in my grasp, to watch my triumphant expression in his mask's reflection.

I edge forward on my perch to get a better look at the Inovarian. Yes, his opaque helmet would be the perfect mirror, much better than the ones looking down at me on that day.

My skull throbs at the memory. I close my eyes to alleviate my budding headache and allow a coolness to wash over me.

When I open them, the foggy air is as green as the foliage that hides me. I run my hands over the tree branch, surprised that it's so smooth. Its texture doesn't matter, though. As long as it shields me from another one of their attacks, I'm content.

The sound of footsteps rips me from my thoughts. An abnormally short Inovarian stalks into my line of sight, likely on her way to meet the larger one a few yards away. Her head moves from left to right as she scans the room. My breath hitches. She must be looking for me!

I grab my blaster to prepare for her attack, determined not to fall victim as my slain comrades have. The little Inovarian bristles in response then starts speed walking. I rise to my feet. She knows!

Of course she does! This must be a trap. She must've seen my teammates and me flee to higher grounds to evade their foot soldiers after the poison rain. She's just playing ignorant so she and her comrades can catch us off guard. I can't help but laugh at their simplicity. I'm much too clever for that.

I rise to my feet and prime my blaster. This ends now. No more Quinzentenians will be dying today.

I aim my gun at the large, well-embellished Inovarian. He's undoubtedly their leader. He dies first, then the little one and whoever else is waiting to ambush us.

"Commander, something isn't right. I think we should g—"

I squeeze the trigger.

The sound of glass shattering softens the pounding in my head. Dull nails dig into my forearms. I look down to see First Recruit Poním clinging to me.

"Commander Unrok, what have you done?"

I ignore the boy's reprimand, focusing on my target instead. The big one is alive. His partner is sprawled on top of him like some kind of shield. She must've protected him from the fatal shot. I draw my weapon again, this time targeting her. It seems that she needs to be taken care of first.

"Captain Minókyt gave us strict orders to stay hidden!" My soldier hisses.

A chill runs down my spine. Yes, the captain did tell my team to stay hidden until she could extract us. I look past my trainee to see my other subordinates peek out from their hiding places with weapons in hand. The sight makes me grin. I may have disobeyed a command, but I know that my team and I can turn the tide in our favor.

"Our cover was already blown," I tell him, priming my second blaster. "So we might as well enjoy ourselves. Target the little one and whoever else shows up. I get the decorated one."

HOW IT'S CHANGED

This passage's unreliable narrator, Commander Unrok, is a war-hardened Quinzentenian soldier with PTSD and residual poisoning. These vivid flashbacks warp his sense of reality, compromise his emotional stability, and misguide his judgment. Unrok discusses the hallucinations and severe chills his ailing comrades suffer from but is unable to identify his identical symptoms. His condition and lack of self-awareness lead him to disobey a direct order and endanger his trainees.

Unrok's team was meant to stay hidden during this boarding mission. The veteran goes as far as reprimanding one of his soldiers for almost blowing their cover, so his strike against Rombag speaks to his sudden bout of irrationality. His trauma and paranoia drove him to attack, which ultimately compromised the entire mission. Unrok's actions initiated the conflict that motivated Mali to take a proactive approach to fighting. Consequentially, his trainees fell victim to her heightened drive to protect her teammates.

This point of view shift not only explains why the firefight occurs but also provides emotional insight into the Inovarian-Quinzentenian war. This rewrite looks past Mali's theoretical assumptions about conflict and dives into its harsh actualities. Many soldiers like Unrok are physically, mentally, and emotionally scarred from their deployment. The veteran is unable to hear loud noises or see an enemy's decorated uniform without being pitched into overstimulating visions. Despite his evident suffering, he prioritizes his comrades by preemptively attacking Rombag in hopes of minimizing casualties. His well-meaning actions were evidentially ruinous, but that goes to show how easily physical and psychological ailments can compromise a person's rationale and credibility.

PART 2
THE EXTERNAL: IT PAYS TO BE ON THE OUTSIDE

Each category of point of view has a different scope. Most first-person narratives are told by characters in the story, while second and third-person works are delivered by speakers who are removed from the plot's events.

These orators' distance from the protagonists lacks the diary-like intimacy of first-person accounts, but this separation does offer more detailed and comprehensive recollections of events since insight deficiencies and personal biases don't limit the audience's access to information. Third-person speakers give us an aerial view of the characters' lives, which provides detailed assessments of the cast's mannerisms and setting. Second-person orators accomplish this same goal but focus on the protagonist's thoughts and project them onto the reader, forcing them to consider how they would fair in similar situations.

These types of commentators allow writers to give us a wider scope of their work, so even if you prefer the immersive nature of first, you still need to know why it pays to narrate from outside your characters' heads.

First-Person Observer POV

——

Whether you'll admit it or not, you're an opinionated people watcher. But don't worry, I won't tell. People are nosey by nature, so if I snitched on you, I'd have to out myself and everyone else. Some of us are admittedly more habitual lookers than others, but at the end of the day, we all take in the world around us and make (hopefully internal) comments. The first-person observer point of view is really just the literary embodiment of our tendency to mind other people's business.

DEFINITION

Stories narrated in the first-person observer (FPO) point of view are told by an individual that is not an active character in the story. These speakers function much like sports broadcasters: They give readers play-by-play plot commentary and provide reactions along the way. FPOs are arguably the most reliable first-person narrators since they quite literally call it how they see it. Their voice and diction set the tone of a work, but they otherwise recall the events how they occurred.

PERSPECTIVE ATTRIBUTES

ATTENTION TO DETAIL

Authors with an affinity for fine details love FPO narrators because these speakers allow them to list the protagonist's features, habits, and mannerisms. Unlike the other first-person points of view, the protagonist is typically a mystery to the storyteller, so the FPO must use their powers of discernment to decode the lead's actions throughout the story. This perspective can at times read like a case study full of theories and failed hypotheses because the speaker is using their observations to make sense of the central character's personality and motivations. A perfect example of an analytical FPO is Sir Arthur Conan Doyle's character Sherlock Holmes.

Though nearly all of Doyle's short stories are narrated in the FPSC POV through Dr. John Watson's eyes, Sherlock himself serves as an FPO through his dialogue. As anyone who's ever read any of Holmes's genius ramblings can tell you, the detective has a talent for observation. Throughout his adventures, Sherlock uses his photographic memory, calculating train of thought, and natural sense of curiosity to animate every case.

Every time I read an instillation of Doyle's series, I'm in awe by the astute assessments and witty humor laced throughout the investigator's speech. By the end of each work, the suspect/protagonist seems like an actual person with realistic wants and motivations. FPO narrators operate in a similar fashion: They use their assessments of the character's disposition and circumstances to identify intriguing patterns and make their own entertaining deductions.

DRAMA

Everyone's at least a little nosey and people-watches from time to time. As my fellow (honest) observers and I will tell you, it's hard to look away when you see or overhear something intriguing. This first-person perspective plays on our natural curiosity and draws us into the drama, making it hard to step away until the scene plays out. Authors do well to capitalize on their audience's messy tendencies by presenting them with unusual premises. Take a look at my short story "Disney Day" for an example of an FPO being nosey while on the clock:

"DISNEY DAY"

Everyone usually takes Disney's "Happiest Place on Earth!" thing seriously, but that doesn't seem to be the case with these two. Throughout my years here, the majority of the couples I've seen are nauseously chipper. They're normally holding hands, smiling, taking selfies, being all lovey-dovey—you know, the whole nine yards—which is why these two look so out of place.

Well, let me rephrase that. *He* belongs here, but she definitely doesn't.

Dude's been talking nonstop since they sat on the bench across from my stand a few minutes ago. He seems like a regular ol' ball of energy, but anyone with half-working eyes can tell that her Happiest Place on Earth is probably her bed, not an amusement park. This lady looks like she's one missed cup of coffee away from flatlining. I'm pretty sure the only thing keeping her upright is his arm around her shoulders.

Her boyfriend's incessant chattering is visibly draining her already strained energy reserves. Poor thing. Despite her palpable exhaustion, she's polite—definitely more than I'd be—and indulges his rambling. For a moment, I doubt that she even hears him, but she covers her eyes when he asks her to, so I guess she's sorta checked in. As she blinds herself, he slips off the bench and gets onto one knee.

I lean forward with a giddy smile. This is gonna be *good*.

She uncovers her face at his prompting.

"Will you marry me?"

Her eyes, which were heavy with fatigue moments ago, widen with shock—and, dare I say, distress?—as her left hand automatically rises to cover her gasp.

"Oh, my *God*. I—oh, God!" is her reaction.

He smiles up at her, ever so pleased to take her by surprise.

It's her third *Oh my God!* that clues me in on her answer before she says it.

She shakes her head no, and his beaming grin dims into a grimace of disbelief. He's too dumbfounded to stand, so he just stays there staring up at her.

I snort. Well, that's gonna be an awkward car ride home.

ANALYSIS

As you likely already know, Disneyland is a very popular proposal site, so much so that the resort ran a Happily Ever After firework show for four years, so couples' attitudes and interactions typically reflect the loving atmosphere (Dufresne, 2021). Anyone outside of that norm is worth noting, so my narrator and readers are inclined to stick around to find out why the duo doesn't blend in with the rest.

Similarly, other authors can dramatize ordinarily joyous locations, events, and situations by having the FPO observe an unconventional interaction. The speaker's vantage point allows them to center the narrative around the protagonist's strange reaction and make the oddity entertaining, whereas other perspectives would focus on the character's internal dialogue during that time.

Beyond the visual aspects of the FPO POV, this perspective is perfect for writers who want an excuse to lavish their text with dark humor. My narrator has a comedic approach to an otherwise awkward and heartbreaking event because he doesn't have any personal stakes in this situation. His distance allows him to crack jokes at the (impending ex-) boyfriend's expense, while any other narrator would have likely taken a more sympathetic tone to his heartbreak. For my fellow authors who are inclined to make jokes out of their own characters' misfortune, I recommend taking the FPO POV for a spin because, realistically, what other perspective lets you poke fun at them without distracting from the plot?

SOCIAL SETTINGS

Unlike the other first-person narrators, the FPO typically doesn't directly interact with the protagonist, nor do they participate in the plot's events. This removed position allows them to understand and present the character's traits in a relatively objective manner. These speakers use their observations, knowledge, and opinions to supplement the discourse around the figure's interactions. FPOs have the unique opportunity to explore the protagonist's relationships in a formulaic manner instead of fixating on the lead's emotions as the other perspectives do.

As explained earlier, FPOs have limited scopes. They don't have direct access to others' thoughts, but their insightful nature compensates for the lack of information. Accounts told in this perspective often read like a lively report or case study because of the narrator's attention to detail. FPOs embody the concept that "actions speak louder than words" since they make most of their commentary based on the protagonist's actions. They pay special attention to the hero's mannerisms and choices to deduce what kind of person they are.

Take my short story "Horrible Hosts," for example:

"HORRIBLE HOSTS"

The Nova Lab and Observatory has been the UN's scientific hub for the past twenty-five years. Hundreds of thousands of scientists have converged on the facility over the years to collaborate on groundbreaking inventions, each feeling at home among the chemicals and circuit boards. Nova is a blissful paradise for theoretical thinkers and tinkerers alike, which is why Councilman Gerard stands out so much.

His signature pastel shirts seem neon in the sea of white lab coats, especially from the cameras here in the security room. Whenever he sits in the cafeteria, his colorful attire becomes both the frame's and fellowships' central focus. The scientists treat him well in these common areas, addressing the politician with polite tones and stiff grins. They would always greet him first, ask about his stay at Nova, and inquire whether or not the UN's finance ministry would expand the observatory's funding.

Gerard only smiles with his teeth during the small talk, evidently energized by the interactions no matter how short-lived they are. The conversation always fizzles out once he tells the researchers that he has to consult with the ministry after his audit is complete and vote before a decision is to be made. Within a few minutes, Nova's residents either leave the councilman where he sits or turn to each other to continue their scientific chatter. The old man always tries his best, but he can never keep from frowning at the dismissal.

I sigh, my expression likely just as pitiful. Maybe interpersonal studies should be a mandated course here. These people are horrible hosts.

ANALYSIS

My narrator, true to their classification, relies on observations to explain Councilman Gerard's relationship with those aboard the Nova Observatory. They show you the social conditions the evidentially extraverted man endures and leave you with enough visual cues to deduce that he feels ignored and isolated. This perspective is perfect for explaining how characters feel in foreign settings, especially when the rules of engagement differ from what they're used to.

ACTION

The FPO POV is great for analyzing the character's reactions to their social environments and showing how they navigate physical settings as well.

As much as I adore the sensationalism of the FPP POV, it often shortchanges readers of the visual aspects of action sequences. These bustling scenes have a lot of moving pieces like complicated technology, flashy pyrotechnics, and awesome stunts that we only catch glimpses of in the protagonist's rush. FPO narrators, on the other hand, have the vantage point to give vivid explanations of what the hero is seeing. They can track the character's movements throughout the scene and comment on their use of setting. I'd rather read an FPO rendition of a fast-paced Transformers-esque robot fight scene with a play-by-play from an invested speaker than the protagonist because either a lot of the action would be cut off or the prose would be flat-out illogical.

The main character realistically wouldn't marvel at their opponent's aesthetics in the middle of a life-or-death situation, so an FPON is a great middle ground for those of us who want those details and animated commentary. The narrator's vantage point allows them to bring attention to the visual aspects of the story, such as costume design and facial expressions, while commenting on the protagonist's agility and combat skills. Just as sports fans relate athletes' statistics to their capabilities, first-person observer narrators also assess the hero's aptitude by studying their mannerisms.

The first-person observer perspective is suited for authors who prefer to show, not tell. Through the narrator's astute analyses, readers are exposed to the physical manifestations of the character's traits, training, and emotions all by watching the protagonist in action. What a perfect perspective for those of us who enjoy the subtleties and theatrics of storytelling!

"The Adventure of the Lion's Mane"

As mentioned earlier, I've nicknamed the first-person observer point of view "the Sherlock POV" because the detective is arguably the keenest investigator in literary history, and FPO speakers are similarly perceptive and insightful. It's only fitting to use excerpts from one of Sherlock's solo adventures, "The Adventure of the Lion's Mane," (1926) to highlight the perks of this perspective.

> At this period of my life the good Watson had passed almost beyond my ken. An occasional week-end visit was the most that I ever saw of him. Thus I must act as my own chronicler. Ah! had he but been with me, how much he might have made of so wonderful a happening and of my eventual triumph against every difficulty! As it is, however, I must needs tell my tale in my own plain way, showing by my words each step upon the difficult road which

lay before me as I searched for the mystery of the Lion's Mane.

I'd like to note that Sir Arthur Conan Doyle's beloved Sherlock series is, for the most part, written in the first-person secondary character POV. Dr. John Watson accompanies the detective during nearly all his adventures and describes what the man is up to. The two develop a close relationship, which gives the doctor the needed context and insights to make sense of the enigma that is Sherlock Holmes. Despite Watson's understanding of his friend, he isn't capable of keeping up with the investigator's hawk-like observational skills and rapid-fire assessments, hence the near-guaranteed monologue in every short story.

"The Adventure of the Lion's Mane" is one of the few instances when the audience gets to see Sherlock solve a case in real time without having to wait for him to backtrack and inform Watson of his findings. Take the following excerpt for example: When scientist Fitzroy McPherson abruptly collapses, his companion Harold Stackhurst freezes at the sudden turn of events while Holmes' mind immediately switches into observation mode.

> My companion was paralysed by the sudden horror of it, but I, as may well be imagined, had every sense on the alert. And I had need, for it was speedily evident that we were in the presence of an extraordinary case. The man was dressed only in his Burberry overcoat, his trousers, and an unlaced pair of canvas shoes. As he fell over, his Burberry, which had been simply thrown round his shoulders, slipped off, exposing his trunk. We stared at

it in amazement. His back was covered with dark red lines as though he had been terribly flogged by a thin wire scourge. The instrument with which this punishment had been inflicted was clearly flexible, for the long, angry weals curved round his shoulders and ribs. There was blood dripping down his chin, for he had bitten through his lower lip in the paroxysm of his agony. His drawn and distorted face told how terrible that agony had been.

Let's take a moment to appreciate the first line of this passage. It beautifully contrasts how a normal person would react to "sudden horror," while Sherlock, apathetic as ever, "had every sense on the alert . . . [for he's] in the presence of an extraordinary case." The detective is one of the best observers in literary history because his trademarked emotional distance allows him to view every tragedy as if it were a puzzle to be solved rather than a life that was just lost.

Not all FPOs are as coldhearted as Holmes, but their detachment from the characters allows them to catch minute details that no other first-person narrator likely would. For example, while Stackhurst is still in shock over McPherson's demise, Sherlock zooms in on the man's injuries and instantly cross-references his knowledge of flogging methodology to make his apt deduction.

I was kneeling and Stackhurst standing by the body when a shadow fell across us, and we found that Ian Murdoch was by our side. Murdoch was the mathematical coach at the establishment, a tall, dark, thin man, so taciturn and aloof that none can be said to have been his friend . . . On one occasion, being plagued by a little dog belonging to McPherson, he had caught the creature up and hurled it through the plate-glass window, an action for which Stackhurst would certainly have given him his dismissal had he not been a very valuable teacher. Such was the strange complex man who now appeared beside us. He seemed to be honestly shocked at the sight before him, though the incident of the dog may show that there was no great sympathy between the dead man and himself.

This description of the ominous Ian Murdoch only works as well as it does because Doyle uses an FPO narrator. Realistically, most speakers, first or otherwise, wouldn't include such a lengthy introduction during such a dire situation—much less talk about the victim's relationship with Murdoch's grouchy lap dog—because it's not immediately important. Sherlock, however, uses his foreknowledge of Murdoch and McPherson's relationship to rule out the mathematician as a suspect.

For the rest of the plot, the other investigators and townspeople try to pin the death on Murdoch because they are too blinded by their biases against the man to see his innocence as Holmes has. This level-headedness and distance from the emotional aspects of the case allow him to find the true killer, *Cyanea capillata*, a deadly fish that stung McPherson while he was swimming.

The first-person observer POV was the perfect choice for "The Adventure of the Lion's Mane" because it lets the detective solve the seemingly straightforward case and gives readers a front-row view of the inner workings of Holmes's mind. Any other first-person account (Watson's or otherwise) would have lacked the objective clarity that only the investigator and narrators of this sort possess. The townspeople's hasty assumptions and partialities would have condemned an innocent man because they do not possess the emotional disconnect and keen observational skills needed to solve the case while providing the same reading experience. A third-person narrator would have the distance and oversight required to give a thorough assessment of the "crime," but they would lack Sherlock's analytic charm.

Authors do well to use FPO narrators because they provide the perfect balance between the first and third-person perspectives. Their observations allow readers to gain a firm understanding of the characters' conflict while also providing entertaining commentary that makes the story feel like a riveting investigation rather than an impersonal aerial view of the protagonist's life.

Incipience First-Person Observer

Poet and best-selling author Dr. Maya Angelou often said, "When someone shows you who they are, believe them the first time" because our observations are often enough to make accurate assessments of others. Despite her claims of pacifism, Mali is willing to bend her ideals when needed, so much so that a third party wouldn't be able to guess that she was so adamantly opposed to war. Quinzentenian Captain Minókyt acts as this unaware figure to provide you with an unbiased first impression of the protagonist based solely on her actions.

CAPTAIN MINÓKYT

Commander Unrok shouldn't have shot at the Inovarian. I gave his team strict orders to stay hidden unless told otherwise, so there *will* be consequences to face later, but I can't deny that the results are quite interesting.

I know all sentient creatures possess an intuition for danger, but one of the humans seems to be keener to hers than the others. She *sensed* the first laser the moment it was shot.

Unlike the majority of her comrades, this young lady evades my soldiers' gunfire with otherworldly grace. She is a flurry of acrobatics that only pauses to return fire.

Her aim is surprisingly accurate for someone who evidently doesn't know how combat works. She consistently shoots at whoever is aiming at her rather than her easiest target. One of my trainees stood on the pillar directly in front of her with his back turned, yet she shot down a soldier in midair because he fired at her first. Any experienced warrior would have secured a guaranteed kill before attempting to hit a moving target, but she takes the inverse approach every time. Either she's a reactive novice or an expert with an eye-for-an-eye mentality. Based on the way she cringes every time her aim rings true, I suspect the former.

No matter the actual answer, the human does quite a bit of damage by her lonesome. By the time the firefight is over, she has shattered one recruit's shoulder, cauterized another's leg, and shot a hole in a soldier's chest. All of these wounds can be easily repaired by our medics, but the fact that she's capable of such destruction is equal parts impressive, intriguing, and concerning.

She's instinctively an excellent marksman, so imagine the harm she'd cause if she honed her skills. I predict she's a proficient combatant, too, if her acrobatics are any indication. Her commanding officer, the Inovarian that Unrok shot, seems to have ordered the humans to march, so I suppose I'll be finding out momentarily.

The soldiers move to depart when the human pauses them with a gesture. She takes off her helmet and extends it toward the Inovarian. Her lips move as she does. I quickly turn on my monitor's sound to catch the rest of her words.

". . . my helmet."

The Inovarian opens his mouth to speak, but no words leave them. He stares at her for quite some time before she hits him in the chest with the helmet. His eyes flutter for a moment before his senses return.

"Take it," she repeats. Her voice is strong. Confident. "I don't need it. You know what I can do, and you've seen how quickly I react. If we're going to help the others, we need to be at our best, right? You need this to be at your prime, but I have enough adrenaline in my system to be good."

Her statement piques my interest. Adrenaline? The chemical is useful for keeping the body moving, but it isn't known for being a clarifying agent. The inverse is true, from what I know.

I make a mental note to ask one of my scientists about adrenaline's effects on the human body. Perhaps the information I have about their kind is outdated.

The Inovarian tries to hand the human back her helmet. I blink, unsure if my eyes are deceiving me. Inovarians are not very agile, so the helmets they wear protect them from the odd shots they are too stiff to dodge. In all my years of service, I have *never* seen any of them voluntarily fight without headgear. I've witnessed some take helmets off of their dying comrades in the heat of battle to ensure their own survival, so his refusal is stupefying.

The rest of his kind would have accepted her offer without hesitation, so why didn't he? Is he a rarity with a conscience? Is he planning on stealing from one of the injured soldiers? Or is she too valuable to risk a fatal injury?

Whatever his motive is, he seems resolved in his rejection. I don't think that matters, though. The human seems determined to arm him. How noble. He must have made quite the impression to make her so willing to risk her life for him.

He tries to hand back the helmet yet again, but she cuts him off. Her voice is sharp and decisive as she speaks. Had I not known better, I would have thought that she was the commanding officer and he was the subordinate by her tone alone. By the way the Inovarian straightens his spine as she talks to him, I'd say that he agrees with my assessment, too.

"Xiomoazi and the Pagis don't have time for this," she says with a stern tone. "We can argue ethics *after* the Quinzentenians are in the brig."

I don't know whether I should be impressed or offended by her declaration.

HOW IT'S CHANGED

"Actions speak louder than words" is a popular phrase because it is for the most part true. Most of us form our opinions of others based on their reactions because those responses are oftentimes a direct reflection of their beliefs and experiences. The first-person observer point of view applies this concept to fiction by characterizing figures solely on word and deed.

This perspective is especially useful for authors who are looking to provide a minimally biased first-person account. Oftentimes, the narrator is unaffiliated with the protagonist, so they're not so blinded by their mental image of the person that they can't see the character for who they are, unlike the other first-person speakers. They instead use their niche expertise and understanding of people to orient their opinions of their subject.

Quinzentenian Captain Minókyt is a fitting figure to give readers a candid take on Mali since the teen exists within the vacuum of the conflict. Without foreknowledge of her pacifistic beliefs and internal conflict, my speaker's commentary is rooted in her professional understanding of warfare and how the cadet's choices, mannerisms, and reactions align with combat conventions. This allows you to see her as the threat that she is instead of the victim or reluctant hero as the FPP and FPSC renditions depict her.

Beyond the accurate representation of Mali's actions, this perspective is the best suited to explain why her final exchange with Rombag is so significant. The cadet and commander focus on what her sacrifice means in terms of logistics since they're still in active combat. Minókyt, on the other hand, sees it for what it is: an act of mutual concern. Her experience with Inovarians contextualize the conversation, shift the tone, and highlight a development that would have otherwise gone unnoticed.

The first-person observer point of view is great for characterizing protagonists in a similar fashion. By using an insightful and analytical third party as a narrator, authors can present their characters' relationships, actions, and development in an entertaining yet minimally biased manner.

Second-Person POV

——

"If you can learn a simple trick, Scout, you'll get along a lot better with all kinds of folks. You never really understand a person until you consider things from his point of view, until you climb inside of his skin and walk around in it."

—ATTICUS FINCH IN *TO KILL A MOCKINGBIRD* BY HARPER LEE

Whether or not you realize it, you read works written in the second person point of view on a daily basis. Your essay prompts, navigation instructions, and favorite recipes are all written in this perspective. Most people don't bat an eye at this POV in nonfiction works, but the second they see it in fiction, it's suddenly unnerving.

The second person POV is essentially the (pre-Charming) Cinderella of perspectives: an overlooked and unjustly slandered treasure. Much like the princess's infamous stepmother, many authors lock the second person POV away in its tower out of misplaced fear or an insufficient understanding of its beauty. If you find yourself with a similar mindset, let this chapter be the fairy godmother to show you second's shining qualities.

DEFINITION

The second person (SP) POV is very similar to the third-person perspective in the sense that both narrator types are uninfluential plot informants. The only difference between the two is the pronouns used: the SP POV uses second person pronouns (you, your, yours, etc.) to describe the main character's experiences while the third-person perspectives use—surprise, surprise—third person pronouns (she, he, they, etc.). From a purely technical standpoint, that's essentially all that sets the two apart, yet readers react to them very differently.

WHY HESITATE WHEN YOU CAN EDUCATE?

The SP POV is a literary rarity because a lot of readers are uncomfortable with being in such close proximity to the text. In third person stories, the audience serves as onlookers who are in no way a part of the cast. Second-person works, on the other hand, project the protagonist's life onto the reader, forcing them to be an active participant in the story. The immersive nature of this POV can be unsettling depending on a text's content. While many are content with reading about the plights of others, they don't want to picture themselves as the lead of tragic or otherwise (conventionally) unpleasant stories. Many writers let these readers' reservations keep them from writing in this perspective, which is quite a shame because the second person point of view is, in my opinion, the most enlightening of the eight.

The SP POV is perfect for giving people a personal tour of someone else's life. While reading, you are made to believe that you are the main character and get to experience their culture firsthand. Take "Blooming" (2020) by Tanya Rey for example. This short story dives into eating disorders, poverty, and divorce culture all through the eyes of a girl on the cusp of her quinceañera, the coming-of-age party she's dreamed about since childhood. I find myself gleaning more from and further empathizing with the protagonist during every reread. My childhood has little to no parallels to the main character's, so it was eye-opening to learn about my essential inverse by taking a walk in the protagonist's shoes.

Similarly, authors who are looking to educate their readers about different lifestyles should seriously consider using a second person narrator. This perspective provides the audience with an intimate understanding of the highlights and drawbacks of different cultures, lifestyles, social classes, and demographics. While we can learn about a character's life by observing them through the other perspectives, the lessons resonate far better when we picture ourselves as the protagonist, which is one of the many reasons I encourage authors to use the second person POV.

This narration style is an excellent educational tool because it operates on the notion that you never really know someone until you've walked a mile in their shoes. This up-close-and-personal perspective lets readers experience others' hardships and hurrahs as the characters do, which allows the text's themes and morals to resonate much better. The other POVs allow us to view such events as plot devices to develop a fictional figure, but this approach to narration makes each lesson hit home because it forces us to ask ourselves "What if that was me?"

THE Y/N EXPERIENCE: WATTPAD HAD A POINT

While this perspective's educational value is definitely one of its shining qualities, it's by no means second's only perk. Anyone who's old enough to remember the fan fiction craze of the early 2010s can tell you that the second person POV was *sensational* across fan forums.

Fiction and pop culture enthusiasts alike flocked to Wattpad, Tumblr, and similar forums to live out their fantasies through Y/N AUs, alternate universe pieces where you substitute your name (Y/N) with the protagonist's, across genres. These fan fictions served as daydream guides for people who wished they could live in fictional worlds or even be a part of their favorite celebrities' lives. Y/N AU authors still reign supreme in some forums because they understand why it's so important to indulge their audience.

Realistically, the average person's odds of tying the knot with a Hollywood A-lister are slim to none, and it's impossible to take a wardrobe to Narnia, so fans' next-best option is to experience such adventures is via literature. Y/N AU writers use their creative savvy, extensive knowledge of their subject area, and familiarity with their fellow enthusiasts' fantasies to create interactive fan fictions.

During my (early) high school 5 Seconds of Summer obsession, I consumed band member x reader AUs like my life depended on it. I spent countless hours immersed in adventures with my favorite artists, and at the end of each story, I'd spam the writer's comments and inboxes with variations of "Omg it felt like I was really there with them!" and "I can't believe this isn't real!" because they did the impossible by lifting me out of my boring afternoon and into the arms of a certain dreamy drummer.

That, my friend, is the power of the second person point of view: It sells people adventures they'd otherwise never be able to have. Even though readers know that they're not physically with the characters, this writing style allows them to still feel as if they were. Their heart skips a beat when there's a jump scare, they cheer when the protagonist wins, they mourn when characters die, they swoon when the romantic lead loves them back, and their stomach churns when tragedies occur.

These stories indulge fans' desire to be close to their unobtainable figure(s) and are met with raging excitement, so authors, why not create works that grant them this accessibility in the first place? This perspective has seen the most success in fan fiction due to its niche demand, but the principles behind its popularity apply to the narration style as a whole.

Every other perspective follows someone else's story, but the second person POV lets the audience take ownership of the narrative from the very beginning. Feed into peoples' desire to be a part of the action: Give them content and characters to imprint on during what feels like their personal journey. Authors, it behooves you to sell your readers the immersion and euphoria that they can't buy anywhere else. Do yourself a favor and take second for a spin.

"The Haunted Mind"

___

Nathaniel Hawthorne is one of the most famous American Romanticists because he produced quality works in great quantity. Hawthorne wrote nearly one hundred short stories throughout his authorial career, but only a handful of those titles are household names.

Works like "Rappaccini's Daughter," "Ethan Brand," and "The Minister's Black Veil," to name a few, often take center stage, while less popular works mill around in the background. "The Haunted Mind" is one such example of an underappreciated brilliant text. This narrative describes the thoughts and sensations an individual experiences before falling asleep. While the plot itself is simple, its poetic cadence and masterful narration make it a remarkable text.

"THE HAUNTED MIND"

Point of view is the foundation of all literature because it sets parameters for stories' diction. When starting a project, authors select a perspective that aligns with the tone they are trying to establish. Hawthorne chose the SP POV for "The Haunted Mind" (1835) because it embodies the contemplative nature of his prose and retains its lyrical flow.

What a singular moment is the first one, when you have hardly begun to recollect yourself, after starting from midnight slumber! By unclosing your eyes so suddenly you seem to have surprised the personages of your dream in full convocation round your bed, and catch one broad glance at them before they can flit into obscurity. Or, to vary the metaphor, you find yourself for a single instant wide awake in that realm of illusions whither sleep has been the passport, and behold its ghostly inhabitants and wondrous scenery with a perception of their strangeness such as you never attain while the dream is undisturbed. The distant sound of a church-clock is borne faintly on the wind. You question with yourself, half seriously, whether it has stolen to your waking ear from some gray tower that stood within the precincts of your dream.

There are thousands of poems, short stories, and essays that explore insomnia, but few are as interactive as "The Haunted Mind." From the first paragraph, the speaker establishes the premise and sets the tone by asking readers to take an introspective glance into our hazy restlessness. This direct request is only made possible by the story's narration style.

While other works can only inspire readers to consider certain topics, the SP POV allows the narrator to directly ask or tell the reader whatever they would like them to ponder. This feature is particularly useful for authors like Hawthorne who would rather focus on the concepts in their story rather than their characters.

The SP POV makes the reader the protagonist. This unique situation allows authors to completely omit some of the character's background by drawing on common experiences. Nearly everyone has woken up mid-dream to a "perception of . . . strangeness" while gaining their bearings, so the narrator doesn't have to give a particularly lengthy explanation of the sensation. The focus of the passage is not to give readers a singular concrete image to share but to make us think back on our own "realm of illusions . . . wondrous scenery."

This open-endedness would not work in any other perspective because the aim of those approaches to fiction is to show what the characters are experiencing. While our reactions to what we read can differ, we should all share the same general mental image by the end of a first- or third-person passage. The SP POV, on the other hand, is set up to let readers cater the imagery to suit whatever they would ordinarily see during their restless moments.

> If you could choose an hour of wakefulness out of the whole night, it would be this . . . Yesterday has already vanished among the shadows of the past; to-morrow has not yet emerged from the future. You have found an intermediate space where the business of life does not intrude, where the passing moment lingers and becomes truly the present; a spot where Father Time, when he thinks nobody is watching him, sits down by the wayside to take breath. Oh that he would fall asleep and let mortals live on without growing older!
>
> Hitherto you have lain perfectly still, because the slightest motion would dissipate the

fragments of your slumber. Now, being irrevocably awake, you peep through the half-drawn window-curtain, and observe that the glass is ornamented with fanciful devices in frostwork, and that each pane presents something like a frozen dream . . .

You sink down and muffle your head in the clothes, shivering all the while, but less from bodily chill than the bare idea of a polar atmosphere. It is too cold even for the thoughts to venture abroad. You speculate on the luxury of wearing out a whole existence in bed, like an oyster in its shell, content with the sluggish ecstasy of inaction, and drowsily conscious of nothing but delicious warmth, such as you now feel again. Ah! that idea has brought a hideous one in its train . . .

"The Haunted Mind" follows a stream of consciousness, meaning that the text ebbs and flows through tones and topics just as the human mind wanders. These paragraphs illustrate just how rapidly an individual's thoughts change direction during their idle moments. This second person narrator seamlessly guides us through these shifts, prompting us to ruminate on each new topic before moving on to the next one. The subjects of this passage flow together seamlessly in such a short space, a feat that would have been difficult if not impossible to pull off so well in any other perspective.

A third-person narrator could achieve this perspective's brevity, but it would lack resonance with the audience. "The Haunted Mind" as is allows readers to picture themselves as the protagonist. They subconsciously use their imagination and personal experiences to create images to go along with the text, effectively creating a scene for them to inhabit throughout each description. Third person narratives, on the other hand, use concrete language and specific details to directly tell readers what the character is thinking, feeling, and, seeing rather than allowing them to picture things themselves.

This distance from the character would make readers feel like they're watching someone else make sense of their insomnia rather than processing restlessness themselves. A first-person narrative would be similarly prescriptive, though it would grant readers a closer look into the character's mind. This proximity would allow them to experience their thoughts in real time, but "The Haunted Mind" would undoubtedly be downright disorienting.

Within the span of three paragraphs, the narrator has us contemplate midnight's classification, Father Time's sway on mortality, the weather, future travel plans, the prospects of staying swaddled in bed forever, and more. If this work was an FPP narrative, Hawthorne would have likely had to expand upon those thoughts and create transitions between them so the text wouldn't feel abrupt. He would have also needed to give the protagonist a personality to inhabit and a background to shape their inner dialogue to make the story worth following.

These additions would have ultimately impeded the prose's intended flow and made the succinct work lengthy. The second-person perspective is the ideal middle ground between the first and third person POV. The distant tone of this text as is works wonderfully since the narrator is guiding us through different subject matters to prompt our own thoughts instead of presenting a character's intimate musings, so the prose requires few personal touches.

"The Haunted Mind" is a poetic and dynamic piece that only works well because of the perspective it is told in. The interactive nature of this text would be completely disrupted had Hawthorne chosen any other narration style. This short story's tone, resonance, and focus would have completely shifted with the introduction of a protagonist other than the reader. "The Haunted Mind" would have been a reflection of an individual's encounter with the haze between the conscious and unconscious rather than a guide to help readers use their imagination to explore their own restlessness as it was meant to be.

"Closed Eye"

The second person point of view has always been the least popular perspective in mainstream publishing. Thankfully, there has been a recent uptake in works printed in this narration style, but it's still rare to find second person pieces and even scarcer to find one with essays published about it. In order to help you further understand the strengths of this POV, I have written the following short story:

"CLOSED EYE"

You've spent your entire life as a rather content wallflower. You've never been one to catch people's eyes, nor have you been the type to draw a crowd. This lack of attention has never bothered you because you enjoy your anonymity. You love being on the fringes of your community because it allows you to exist outside of the hierarchy and strife that your colleagues constantly complain about. Unfortunately, your unique contentment has escaped you for the past month. You were yanked from your quiet post as a research lab guard to help with an interstellar expedition trip.

You ordinarily like space travel, but this rendezvous has you on edge. There are cameras covering every square inch of the place save for the bathrooms. You went from a faceless guard to a lab rat under a magnifying glass overnight, and you *despise* this change of events. You can feel the camera's lenses roaming over your skin day in and day out. It feels like you're never alone even when you are. You try not to think about it too much, but it's hard to ignore the unnerving sensation of being knowingly observed.

Your weary soul only gets respite when you're in the restroom, the one place without cameras, but other than that, you're under a lens 24-7, even in your sleep. There's a security camera on your ceiling, and you hate it with a passion. It's dim and easy to ignore for most, but not you. Its blinking green light lets you know that someone's watching on the other side. The flashes remind you of a lone omniscient eye: eerie, all seeing, ever watching.

You have to sleep with the covers pulled over your head or else you'll stare down the Eye until your next shift starts. Your roommate Morgan thinks that it's ironic that a security guard like yourself hates when others look at you when it's your job to do the same. You always reply, "I prefer when surveillance is a one-way street."

Even though you're not a fan of crowds, you gravitate toward them during your free time so you don't feel singled out by the cameras. You know that the operators in the observation room rarely if ever zoom in on packed spaces, so you only feel out of sight among the masses. You always volunteer to guard the ship's busiest lab, take all of your breaks in the mess hall during rush hour, and avoid working lull hours as much as possible. Unlike your reclusive coworkers, you hate when you're assigned sparsely populated, late-night security sweeps and do your best to trade shifts with one of the hermit officers.

Unfortunately, the ship has a skeleton crew tonight, so you're stuck roaming the eerie halls by yourself. Yesterday, the sensors picked up an undiscovered tropical planet. After scanning the surface and deeming the uninhabited world safe, the captain decided to let the crew have a look around. Unluckily for you, there are only a handful of other officers that have to guard the ship while everyone else has fun. You're more begrudging than usual walking your route tonight.

As you pad down the hallways, you sense that the cameras feel . . . different. Like there are more of them somehow. The sensation of being watched is much more intense than usual. You typically feel the ship's Eyes roaming over you, but today they're burning holes into your back. Halfway through your route, you call the observation department to ask if they've added any new devices. They laugh at the question, well aware of your camera shyness, before telling you that they haven't. Your face warms with indignation, but that doesn't compare to the gaze digging into your skin.

You do your best to quell the swirling uneasiness in your stomach until you hear a rasp from behind you. It sounds like someone's breathing hard but they're trying to be quiet. The first time your ears catch the sound, you try to tell yourself it's nothing. The second time makes your skin crawl because the panting sounds almost wet. The third time the wheezing is so loud that it *echoes*. The reverberating gasp causes your anxiety to flare.

You call the observation deck again.

"Taylor," the surveillance officer sighs, your distress no longer amusing. "There's no one in the halls with you. The maintenance team is working on the leaks in the vents, so that's the whistle you've been hearing."

"But it's not a whistle," you reply. "It's a *rasp*. There's a difference."

"Whistle, rasp, wheeze, whatever it is, it's just the ship. Scout's honor."

Despite the monitor's reassurance, you call every fifteen minutes for the next four hours of your patrol. The department stops answering after your third time, but that doesn't stop you from trying.

Once your shift is over, you head straight to your room. You lock the main door behind you, dash into your bathroom, and lock that too. In your haste, you don't notice that your typically pristine room has drawers askew, beds unmade, and trinkets misplaced, nor do you notice that the green Eye is closed. All you're concerned about is being *alone*, out of sight.

You sit down on your bathroom floor with your knees drawn to your chest for nearly an hour, enjoying the feeling of the plush rug in still silence. You are shaken from your serenity when the bathroom door jingles. You try and fail to remember hearing your roommate come in, but you reason that you were lost in thought. Besides, your shipmates should be returning from their overnight on the planet, right?

The door handle jingles again. You tell your roommate that you'll be out in a second. The shaking intensifies. You let out a huff of annoyance as you rise to your feet. You reach to unlock the door when you hear the same rasping from earlier. This time it's heavier, guttural even.

"Morgan?" You ask hesitantly. Your hand hovers over the knob.

The panting slowly turns into a feral growl. The pit in your stomach churns so hard that you gag. You dial the observation dispatcher from your holo-watch. This time your call goes through. There's a wet pant on the other side of the line accompanied by pained groans in the background.

You correctly deduce that the planet isn't uninhabited after all.

ANALYSIS

The second person POV is an excellent narration choice for mystery and horror authors. Much like a third-person narrator, a second person speaker is more aware of the protagonist's conflict and surroundings than the character is. This knowledge differential is good for foreshadowing, creating tension, and drawing attention to the story's setting. "Closed Eye" uses these three perspective attributes in the opening paragraphs to establish the short story's premise and explain the main character's personality.

Taylor hates being observed to the point that our lead never feels truly alone or at peace at any point throughout the story. This conflict leaves readers to wonder whether the protagonist is paranoid until the narrator points out the Eye—ceiling camera—is out and the room is in disarray, an observation that Taylor fails to make. This detail allowed me to succinctly reestablish guard's credibility, drum up tension, and provide an Easter egg for viewers to stumble upon.

If I were to rewrite this short story in any other perspective, the foreshadowing elements wouldn't have been as subtle. As is, the narrator uses the Eye as an unsettling warning sign that comes full circle. Readers initially don't know that it will serve as an indication that something went wrong because it's just an example of one of the many things that disturbs Taylor's peace.

If "Closed Eye" were narrated from the third person POV, the speaker likely would have hinted that the Eye would be a pivotal detail, causing readers to be on the lookout for it. Had I written this in the FFP perspective, Taylor wouldn't have noticed the inert light at all, and the jingling doorknob would have been a complete surprise. Until the guard opens the door, my audience and protagonist alike won't factually know "that the planet isn't uninhabited after all." Even though this piece ends in a slight cliffhanger, my readers get the closure of knowing that Taylor's instincts were spot on even if they don't know what happens next.

Beyond the dramatic applications, this perspective is useful for creating a unique reading experience. As explained earlier, the second person POV can be used to project a new existence onto the audience. While immersed in a passage, an individual is supposed to imagine what their life would be like if they were born into a different race, class, sex, nationality, etc. as they peel through the plot. I'd like to note that the inverse is true as well.

The second-person perspective is popular for self-insert works. This essentially means the author can choose not to describe their character's physical attributes so that the reader can picture themselves as the protagonist more easily. I purposefully chose gender-neutral names and omitted pronouns and demographic-specific details to

- (a) make it easier for readers to picture themselves as the lead

- (b) focus on the mystery at hand

Had I provided Taylor with a physical profile, I would have ultimately distracted from the plot because the character's race, gender, ethnicity, body type, etc. have virtually nothing to do with the story's events. Such details would have obstructed the prose's flow, detracted from the central aim, and integrated the reader's bias into the story. If I had penned Taylor as a young Afro-Latina or a middle-aged Cantonese man, my audience would have been inclined to use their understanding of the character's background to judge the guard's actions and attitude. By omitting demographics altogether, Taylor is instead a blank slate for the reader to inhabit throughout this adventure.

Incipience Second-Person POV

There are thousands of heist and espionage stories because a lot of us enjoy following conventionally villain-esque people throughout their adventures. It's fun to watch them take a walk on the wild side since for those of us law-abiding citizens, it's our only chance to experience the misdeeds for ourselves. These nefarious missions are entertaining to watch as third parties looking in, but they're much more amusing when we get to be the villains ourselves.

The second person point of view lets readers experience being good at being bad without the associated guilt of committing the crimes in real life. Since *Incipience*'s protagonist is a conventionally heroic figure, this rendition follows Poním, a Quinzentenian who's having a jolly ol' time while everyone is fighting for their lives.

PONÍM

As fellow anthropoids, the humans resemble you in many respects. Their limbs can move as yours do, but they lack Quinzentenian grace. They move about as if their feet are tethered to the ground by chains instead of the ship's (comparatively) nonexistent gravity. Their lumbering movements are one of the few reasons you weren't initially all that concerned when Commander Unrok blew your cover. Sure, there would be consequences to pay when the captain learns what he had done, but as far as you're concerned, that's not your problem.

According to protocol, you have to back him up in his decisions, so it's not as if you'll be reprimanded for following a direct order. Besides, shooting at the humans remedies your boredom, so you welcome the excitement.

At first, it's fun to target the tiles around their feet and watch them scurry out of harm's way. Many of them come close to tripping over their clunky boots, the thick material keeping them from pivoting as well as your battle flats allow you to. Their rushed movements and inability to assess their situation keep a smile drawn across your lips. As your unit's highest-ranking marksman, you could've taken out all the humans by now if you truly wanted to. Never one to spoil your own fun, you continue playing your game to pass the time.

Commander Unrok pauses his assault on the Inovarian to contact you through the comms system. "Poním, handle the humans!"

The older man's tone tells you that *handle* is synonymous to *kill*. You ignore his request for three reasons: you enjoy seeing them dance about; Captain Minókyt would demote you for eliminating anyone other than an Inovarian unless absolutely necessary; and harming the incompetently trained group would feel like assaulting children.

Well, to be more precise, all but one of the humans are infantile combatants. You've nicknamed her Enigma because she's the only Earthling who can keep with the Inovarian and your fellow Quinzentenians. The outlier has managed to dodge your comrades' shots with remarkable agility, a difficult feat since they're aiming to demobilize her.

As intriguing as she is, you've wisely decided to stay out of her way. The other fifteen humans haven't been able to touch you all, but she's already shot down one of your teammates. Surprisingly, she could have gotten more, if that was her aspiration. You notice that Enigma only targets those who either aim at her first or harm a human. Had she been a properly trained soldier (or half-competent opportunist), she would have killed you when you accidentally turned your back to her while toying with one of her comrades just now. You say a prayer thanking Pekema Ima for the vengeance that blinds her.

You shoot at the air next to one of your toys' head. He, of course, dodges, and you aim at the next in your line up to give him a moment's respite. You turn in time to see Enigma gun down Yrazék. The man his the floor with a *thump!* You flinch at the sound. There's no way he didn't break or rupture something during that fall.

With Yrazék down, half of your unit is incapacitated. Judging by the vigor in which Enigma and her leader are moving, there may be less of you soon.

You swing over to Commander Unrok who's still trying to kill the surprisingly resilient Inova native.

"Commander, we need to retreat," you say.

The only response you receive is a crass string of curses and an order to keep shooting. His response makes your hair stand on end. Before boarding, this man had lectured you for an hour about the importance of understanding your limitations, and now he's bucking the safest course of action?

Your thoughts are pulled from his bizarre response and back to the conflict as you see yet another of Enigma's victims fall. Your throat tightens at the sight of Míkuvyo's bubbling flesh. A few inches over and she would have been dead. If you can't get her help in time, she likely will be.

"Commander!" You plead.

"Not until the Inovarian's dead!"

You two are the only Quinzentenians standing, but that may not be true for much longer. Unrok is drawing the Inovarian's fire while the rest humans are focused on you. You're a superb acrobat and do well dodging, but your skill can't defy all odds. They'll get you soon enough at this rate. You know that you can't keep this up for much longer, so you won't.

In a fluid motion, you grab concussive smoke bombs from your pocket and toss them at the feet of your favorite toy. You watch as it throws the human through the air. The Earthling's figure is soon lost in the haze.

You immediately make for the exit. If Commander Unrok has any sense, he'll follow and reprimand you later. If not, he'll end up like the others, if not worse, given his assailant. Either way, you need to survive long enough to rally reinforcements to save Míkuvyo and the others before it's too late.

You feel his presence behind you once you're in the hallway rafters.

"That cowardice will be on your record," he growls.

"As will your disobedience. I am content with receiving a demerit, but Captain Minókyt may take you before the throne."

You expect the smack on the head, but that doesn't mean it hurts any less.

HOW IT'S CHANGED

It's one thing to give your audience an ambivalent character to follow, but it's a whole different ball game when you make them become that figure. The second person POV projects the protagonist's life on to you, which gives you a deeper understanding of the (anti)hero's life and promotes empathy.

Poním is by all means a sadist. He enjoys making the cadets run for their lives because it beats boredom and is a bit smug when pondering over his ability to snipe them. These traits are conventionally villainous, but he doesn't present as badly as he should because of my choice in perspective. Despite his affinity for cruelty, his rationale and personal set of boundaries make him a redeemable and—dare I say?—likable character even if he's a morally gray one.

This combination operates so well together because people often focus more on the feeling that the author creates around the character than the character's exact words. The sharpshooter's humorous tone is more prominent than his underlying message in large part because readers are naturally inclined to focus on the positive attributes of the character that is supposed to represent them.

If you're looking for a perspective that can allow you to subvert nefarious notions in your texts, you may want to give the second person POV a chance. It's arguably the best suited to teach your audience about different mentalities, lifestyles, and cultures, so take it for a spin and compare its resonance with your drafts in the other perspectives. This narration style is growing more popular by the day because writers are starting to see that it offers a unique and impactful reading experience for their audience that helps them further invest in the prose. Do yourself a favor and give second a chance because it's better to be ahead of the curve than behind!

Third-Person Limited POV

A well-made biographical documentary leaves its viewers with the impression that they know the subject well. Audiences can't help but feel familiar with the film's star because the narrator has provided them with intimate and endearing details about that person's life. The third-person limited point of view is no different. This perspective acts as a camera that follows the protagonist and shows us who they are through a relatively objective yet personable lens.

DEFINITION

Stories told in the third-person limited (TPL) point of view are narrated by individuals who are not characters in the story. These speakers function just like cameras: they document the protagonist's actions in an intriguing manner that ultimately shapes how we view the character, but they don't explicitly state any of their opinions. TPLNs simply present the lead's thoughts and actions and highlight details that the star may not notice. This includes (but is not limited to) descriptions of other character's behavior, well-placed Easter eggs, and misleading speech.

Scope aside, it's very important to note that due to the nonpartisan nature of this POV, the author's diction sets the work's tone. Writers must choose their words carefully to create their desired mood and establish each character's personality.

PERSPECTIVE ATTRIBUTES

OBJECTIVITY AND TRUSTWORTHINESS

Third-person narrators are essentially the GPS system of stories: detached yet reliable voices whose sole purpose is to guide the reader through the plot. Much like a navigation system, you can take TPL speaker's words at face value because their primary objective is to inform you. Granted, they can both be a bit circuitous if you don't set them up correctly, but their words are factually true and will take you where you need to go. Their descriptions of the main character's thoughts, actions, and feelings are accurate to where the figure is in their development and oftentimes hints at where they're going.

TPL speakers are great for authors who want their readers to have a reliable and comprehensive narrative to follow. These orators' distance from the text allows them to litter it with figurative language that helps us make sense of the plot's cast. Their use of metaphors, similes, and analogies create clear imagery that orient us in the characters' personalities, oftentimes without imposing an opinion on us throughout these descriptions. This gives us the chance to experience a nonpartisan, unmediated version of the characters that is unmarred by biases. The TPL perspective not only provides a trustworthy account of the figures' personalities but also gives us an insightful view of the overall plot as well.

FORESHADOWING

Readers often know more about the plot than the hero does in third person accounts. TPLNs have the scope necessary to give us the inside scoop and use foreshadowing to give us a taste of what's to come before the big reveal.

TPL speakers are able to highlight the details that the protagonist misses, like a suspicious onlooker or a seemingly trivial object in the background that tells readers that that character or item will somehow play a pivotal role in the story somewhere down the line. Authors do well to provide their audience with treasure hunts of this sort because they draw fans deeper into the narrative. As readers speculate how that figure or element will affect the hero's journey, they become increasingly interactive with and invested in the mysterious plot placed before them.

TPL speakers are great riddlers and are equally useful as dramatists. TPLNs have the unique ability to blatantly tell their audience the character's fate. Phrases like "Little did she know," "She would come to find," and "Unbeknownst to her" are all very popular phrases in these works because writers love to exploit the dramatic irony that the third person offers. Even though we know what's going to happen, we can't help but feel anxious as we wait for the unsuspecting hero to fall prey to the author's trap.

PLOT TWIST: THE SHOW GOES ON

There are countless ways writers can puppeteer their protagonist into miserable situations no matter what perspective they choose, but it's arguably the most intriguing in the third-person limited POV. As stated earlier, TPL speakers are not characters in the story. They are physically, emotionally, and existentially separate from the plot of the story they narrate. Due to the detached nature of TPLNs, there's no guarantee that the main character lives to see the last page.

Third person stories have the freedom to kill the protagonist because the narrator can continue speaking about the events surrounding their demise. These works are suspenseful because the figure's fate is sincerely unknown until the very last sentence. The show can and will go on without its star, so the question "Will it have to?" is an ever-present query lingering in the background of every third person text, especially ones with volatile settings.

This tension works perfectly in the TPL POV because fans spend an entire plot line emotionally investing in a single character's physical, emotional, and intellectual growth. Readers spend pages drawing close to them, so when authors unexpectedly kill the protagonist, readers feel as if the rug is pulled from under their feet. As my fellow book-lovers can attest, it's sad to see a personable character go when you see it coming, but it's downright heart-wrenching to lose them out of the blue. Creatives do well to leverage the fatal aspects of this perspective to craft memorable scenes and generate emotional responses from their viewers.

The third-person limited point of view is perfect for authors who love to keep their audience on the edge of their seats. The astute insights, unique foreshadowing elements, and unpredictable nature of this perspective create a theatrical and suspense-filled reading experience for viewers.

"The Story of an Hour"

"The Story of an Hour" (1894) by Kate Chopin never fails to make me laugh because it is such a morbidly cheeky tale. This nineteenth-century short story is still popular to date due to Chopin's masterful use of foreshadowing, vivid imagery, and plot twists through her third-person limited narrator.

"The Story of an Hour" plays on the reader's misconceptions about protagonist Louise Mallard's affections for her husband as she reacts to his death. As seen below, Chopin's TPLN's observations are free from emotionally ascribing words, which allows readers to draw conclusions about Louise's heart condition.

> Knowing that Mrs. Mallard was afflicted with a heart trouble, great care was taken to break to her as gently as possible the news of her husband's death.
>
> It was her sister Josephine who told her, in broken sentences; veiled hints that revealed in half concealing. Her husband's friend Richards was there, too, near her. It was he who had been in the newspaper office when intelligence of

the railroad disaster was received, with Brently Mallard's name leading the list of "killed." He had only taken the time to assure himself of its truth by a second telegram, and had hastened to forestall any less careful, less tender friend in bearing the sad message.

She did not hear the story as many women have heard the same, with a paralyzed inability to accept its significance. She wept at once, with sudden, wild abandonment, in her sister's arms. When the storm of grief had spent itself she went away to her room alone. She would have no one follow her.

There stood, facing the open window, a comfortable, roomy armchair. Into this she sank, pressed down by a physical exhaustion that haunted her body and seemed to reach into her soul.

Most people can relate to the distinct heartbreak of losing a loved one and the heap of sorrow that comes with it. Given our shared miseries, this morbid situation would warrant and evoke empathy from most of us if Louise's reaction to her widowing wasn't so odd. While the other railroad disaster widows start at the first of the five stages of grief—denial, Louise immediately skips to stage five, acceptance, believes her sister's words, and begins mourning. This, as the narrator notes, is an abnormal response, which shifts our sympathy to suspicion in an instant. This wariness is only furthered by the flash flood brevity of her tears and the passage to follow:

She sat with her head thrown back upon the cushion of the chair, quite motionless, except when a sob came up into her throat and shook her, as a child who has cried itself to sleep continues to sob in its dreams.

She was young, with a fair, calm face, whose lines bespoke repression and even a certain strength. But now there was a dull stare in her eyes, whose gaze was fixed away off yonder on one of those patches of blue sky. It was not a glance of reflection, but rather indicated a suspension of intelligent thought.

There was something coming to her and she was waiting for it, fearfully. What was it? She did not know; it was too subtle and elusive to name. But she felt it, creeping out of the sky, reaching toward her through the sounds, the scents, the color that filled the air.

Now her bosom rose and fell tumultuously. She was beginning to recognize this thing that was approaching to possess her, and she was striving to beat it back with her will— as powerless as her two white slender hands would have been.

When she abandoned herself a little whispered word escaped her slightly parted lips. She said it over and over under her breath: "free, free, free!" The vacant stare and the look of terror that had followed it went from her eyes. They stayed keen and bright. Her pulses beat fast, and the coursing blood warmed and relaxed every inch of her body.

She did not stop to ask if it were or were not a monstrous joy that held her. A clear and exalted perception enabled her to dismiss the suggestion as trivial.

Call me old-fashioned if you will, but "free, free, free!" doesn't sound like mourning to me.

Louise's reaction is hands down my favorite literary plot twist of all time because it's jaw-droppingly *brilliant*. Like most first-time readers, I initially interpreted her actions according to my own experiences with and understanding of grief. I believed that the widow's sporadic sobs were the beginning phases of bereavement-induced depression. Imagine my surprise when Louise starts cheering to herself! I instantly reread the first half of the short story to find the hints I had missed that foreshadow this event then had a hearty laugh once I caught Chopin's clues.

"The Story of an Hour" is only able to elicit this kind of interactive and awed reaction because of Chopin's narration style. Had the author chosen any other narrator, Louise's excited repetition of "free, free, free!" would have been unsurprising—and debatably revolting—since I would have learned about her feelings immediately upon her widowing. Other points of view might have touched on the sensationalism, but they would have botched the remarkable tone shift, lacked the distance needed to provide vivid imagery, and spoiled this surprise that Chopin's keen-eyed yet unassuming TPLN provides:

> She arose at length and opened the door to her sister's importunities. There was a feverish triumph in her eyes, and she carried herself unwittingly like a goddess of Victory. She clasped her sister's waist, and together they descended the stairs. Richards stood waiting for them at the bottom.

Some one was opening the front door with a latchkey. It was Brently Mallard who entered, a little travel-stained, composedly carrying his grip-sack and umbrella. He had been far from the scene of accident, and did not even know there had been one. He stood amazed at Josephine's piercing cry; at Richards' quick motion to screen him from the view of his wife.

But Richards was too late.

When the doctors came they said she had died of heart disease—of joy that kills.

The TPL speaker only directly mentions her heart condition once before the final scene, choosing to ignore her affliction until the very end of the passage. Louise's sudden death is momentarily jarring to readers before we realize that her demise was preordained from the very beginning. The narrator warned us that others treated her delicately to prevent causing the protagonist any harm, so her death is retrospectively fitting and ragingly ironic since the discovery of her husband's survival killed her rather than his death.

Authors who share Chopin's cheeky affinity for foreshadowing are wise to use the TPL POV as she has. Throughout this short but well-crafted piece, Chopin uses her narrator's neutral voice to leverage readers' misconceptions of Louise's actions, foreshadow plot twists, and orchestrate an ironic yet fitting ending.

Incipience Third-Person Limited POV

─────

As anyone who enjoys westerns and crime TV can tell you, people spend a lot of time ducking for cover during shootouts. When the smoke clears, the main character only has bits and pieces of what happened because they were too focused on trying to protect themselves to see what occurred. This is one of the many reasons that shows of this short are filmed on regular production cameras instead of GoPros. Many authors prefer to use the third-person limited POV to narrate their action scenes for similar reasons.

Unlike most people, Mali's abilities allow her to remain out in the open during battle without getting hurt. Not every action piece follows extraordinary individuals like her, so this TPL rendition of *Incipience* follows Reese, a non-meta-human Izedi, who navigates the firefight to show how this perspective works well with high-energy scenes.

REESE
With five years of amateur boxing under his belt and a house full of brothers, Reese knows a thing or two about pugilism.

He has a mean left hook and an even nastier right, but as the old saying goes, you can't bring fists to a firefight, so the cadet is at a bit of a loss. Pulling a gun isn't his first instinct, so his response time leaves things to be desired. Reese's brain starts buffering the second Commander Rombag gets shot. Unlike the rest of his friends, it takes him a minute to get his bearings and fire back.

Behind his mask, his face blanches. His reflexes were his pride and joy during his time in the ring, so his slow reaction is a chunk off his shoulder. It doesn't help that he only thought to activate his sensors a few seconds before Commander tells Miss Golden Girl—Charlie? Amelia? Maddie? Reese never gets it right—to turn hers on.

The Pagi recruit hasn't had as much battle training as the Izedis, so she has an excuse for her ignorance, but what's his? He was promoted from her team to this one last month, so it's not like he hasn't had time to learn the features. Still, no amount of simulations or suit tutorials could prepare someone to see their seemingly infallible leader get gunned down out of the blue, so he decides to give himself some grace since the Quinzentenians obviously won't.

The aliens have the high ground and are taking full advantage of it. They flip, twist, and leap between the ceiling rafters to corral their targets around the cafeteria. Reese dives, ducks, and dodges out of harm's way to the best of his ability, feeling much like a rat caught in a cat's crosshairs. He can sense that his adversaries are toying with him and the other humans, and that realization makes his chest pound more than the thought of being shot does. He knows they can—will—kill him after they have their fun. After all, the Quinzentenians aren't fighting; they're playing.

From the few glimpses he's seen of them, Reese thinks that Commander Rombag and the Pagi unit girl he brought along seem to be the only real contenders from their team. While he and the other Izedis are struggling to stay out of harm's way, she maneuvers through the onslaught of lasers as if she's performing a well-practiced routine. The teen combines her acrobatic talents to evade danger and returns fire with the same fluidity their enemies possess. In Reese's opinion, that makes her the biggest threat in the room.

As if to prove his point, she shoots a moving target out of the air. The Quinzentenian lands with a loud *thud!* on top of one of the downed Izedis. The sight makes Reese's skin crawl. Even after enduring the Inovarians' bloody training simulations, he has a weak stomach when it comes to wounds, so it isn't a surprise that the sizzling hole in alien's chest makes him want to run the other way. Luckily for him, he doesn't have time to dwell on the imagery.

One of the two remaining Quinzentenians throws a smoke bomb right in front of Reese. The combustion and bursting gas knock the young man off his feet and through the air. His brain pinballs in his skull the second his helmet hits the floor. The impact rattles the cadet enough for him to forget the threat at hand and combat decorum. His limbs relax in their sprawled-out position as his mind hums with white noise. Lying on the hazy cafeteria's floor, Reese resembles a starfish in a murky tide pool instead of the prim and proper Izedi he's been trained to be.

The young man only snaps out of his mildly concussed daze when he feels two fingers on his neck. It takes a few blinks, but he refocuses enough to register that the Pagi girl is checking his pulse.

"I'm alive," Reese says. He tries to sit up, but she puts her hand on his chest, guiding him back to the scorched tile.

"Barely," she replies. "You were out of it for a while. Just stay still, okay?"

Her question doesn't warrant a reply, but if it did, she wouldn't get one. Reese's remaining brain cells are too busy focusing on her touch to formulate a response. How can someone snap from deadly assailant to delicate nurse so quickly? Charmaine's (as he believes her to be) fingers pressed her blaster's trigger as easily as they take his pulse. Reese marvels at the contrast. This girl is built for war.

HOW IT'S CHANGED

Mali's body runs on autopilot when her powers are activated. Her reflexive fighting style doesn't require much thought, so she has the freedom to survey her surroundings. Lest they have a buffer as she does or they are a born-and-raised career soldier like Rombag, the average person doesn't have this privilege. Authors who understand this often-ignored fact of life make their first-person accounts reflect their characters' limitations.

As my fellow speculative fiction writers can tell you, third-person narrators work exceptionally well for showing readers what the characters are experiencing during action scenes. The speaker's distance from the plot gives them the freedom to litter the prose with colorful assessments of the character's predicaments, mannerisms, and gestures. For example, Reese likely wouldn't describe himself as "rat caught in a cat's crosshairs" or a "starfish in a murky tide pool" because his appearance is out of his scope and beyond his concern.

Authors who are interested in putting a similarly playful spin on their fast-paced scenes should consider trying their hand at this perspective. First and second person narrators have to align their speech to fit the character's mood because their stories are rooted in the protagonist's emotions. Third-person multiple and omniscient speakers constantly switch diction and tones to differentiate between characters, so it's difficult to maintain a single mood, much less a humorous one.

The TPL orators, on the other hand, serve as uninvolved onlookers for a single figure. This gives them the wiggle room to make creative analogies and poke fun at the main character's thoughts, actions, and interactions in a way that other narrators can't. Writers who want to experiment with their prose's delivery should try their hand at the third-person limited point of view because it allows them to create an atmosphere for their audience that differs from the protagonist's mood.

Third-Person Multiple POV

───

In life, there are two sides and an ideal present in every story: yours and theirs, and the hope that the truth is somewhere in the mix of things. Two people who experience the same event can have drastically different recollections of the facts due to their distinctive personalities, backgrounds, interests, and worldviews. In court, investigative teams combat this inconsistency by subpoenaing witnesses to accredit the plaintiff or defendant's statements.

In fiction, authors add supporting characters to provide credibility. The third-person multiple point of view is the best equipped to showcase the unpredictable nature of perception because it allows readers to hear the testimonies of as many characters as the author can feasibly manage. Each character's narrative adds to the audience's understanding of the plot by filling in holes that would have otherwise remained gaping had a single person been the sole focus of the story. The third-person multiple POV is the mosaic of fiction: By giving us each character's story, we get to see the bigger picture.

DEFINITION

Stories narrated in the third-person multiple (TPM) POV follow a minimum of two characters throughout the story's plot. In works of this sort, there may not be one definitive protagonist if the author chooses to use each figure as a puzzle piece to give a well-rounded account of a single event, conflict, or location. In other cases, the main character gets the spotlight for the better half of the work, and the secondary characters' accounts are sprinkled in as supplementary information or to juxtapose the lead's actions and traits.

No matter which route writers choose to take, all these figures must have their own distinct voice. Each character's individuality should contribute unique insights and opinions to enhance the audience's working understanding of the conflict and theme. Otherwise, they should serve as side characters since they don't add anything noteworthy to the story. Authors typically give each figure a distinctive personality, background, subplot, arc, and interests to ensure everyone's worldview differs enough to be equal parts educational and distinguishable.

While it is quite popular for the characters to be from varying and at times directly opposing lifestyles, the inverse is also true. Characters don't have to be drastically different in every respect to contribute to the story. The TPM POV is often used to show how people of similar backgrounds can live very different lives, so they can share commonalities as long as their voices don't blend together. Just as a choir director knows how to harmonize their baritones to create rich, low tones, a good TPM author knows how to layer their character's unique voices to create a cohesive story. This is often achieved by connecting the figures either thematically or through the plot.

One of the core requirements of the TPM POV is that everyone must share some sort of connection. There are several approaches to achieving this, such as characters having either similar or opposing experiences with the same conflict, location, culture, relationship, etc. Whatever is chosen to stitch these characters together, the line of filiation should create a cohesive story that readers can keep track of. It's worth noting that the more characters featured in a work, the harder it is to keep track of them all.

Take Marlon James' *A Brief History of Seven Killings* (2014) for example. Though the book isn't exclusively in the third person, the Man Booker Prize-winning work still serves as a fitting example. The nearly seven-hundred-page novel has approximately fourteen characters (more if you count some of their sub-personalities and aliases). While James does an exquisite job individualizing them, it's hard to remember who did what, who's crossed paths, and when things occurred because that's a lot of people and plot lines to keep track of. Even if writers can create lively people worth following as he has, they should be mindful of how much their readers can realistically juggle all at once.

HIGHLIGHTS AND CHARACTERISTICS

THE BUTTERFLY EFFECT

Whether we choose to acknowledge it or not, our personalities, worldviews, and socioeconomic standings are primarily dependent on our environments since our communities dictate who and what we encounter. Our collectives shape us into who we are and determine what we put into the world.

All societies operate on the Butterfly Effect, meaning that our actions, big or small, can and will influence someone else's life whether or not we know them. The third-person multiple POV best mimics this phenomenon because each character's storyline either directly or indirectly shapes another character's arc. This perspective is perfect for showing the interconnectivity of individuals on social, political, financial, and interpersonal levels.

My favorite instance of the TMP's interconnectivity is *There There* (2018) by Tommy Orange. This hybrid narrative uses the TMP POV (with sprinkles of first and second when needed) to follow twelve characters who converge at a powwow in Oakland, California. The dozen share some commonalities like their demographic (they're all Native People), family ties, and a relationship with Oakland, but beyond that, they are very different people whose lives and interests ordinarily wouldn't overlap.

Despite their laundry list of dissimilarities, every character still manages to directly or indirectly push another figure to attend the powwow, resulting in everyone interacting by the close of the novel. Orange masterfully weaves the twelve's stories together like a tapestry, each arc perfectly intertwining to create an impressive image for readers to marvel at.

Just as Orange's characters all contribute to the story's climax in one way or another, writers can use the TPM POV to give readers a holistic understanding of what is happening throughout the plot. This perspective shows us the story from every angle and arguably provides more of a thorough explanation of events than any other POV allows.

While the first and second person narratives focus on one character's understanding of the story, the TMP POV gives in-depth insights from multiple characters, supplying readers with ample testimonies to piece together the truth for themselves. The other third-person perspectives are more insightful than the first and second, but the scope and pacing associated with the two don't allow for as much detail as the TPM perspective does.

For example, the TPL POV is known for hovering over one character for the entire work, pointing out what the protagonist has failed to notice, but it doesn't have the power to go into depth about what other characters do behind the scenes to shape the story's outcome. The third-person omniscient (TPO) perspective does have the scope needed to give readers ample information, but works of this sort typically flit between characters so quickly that we don't get a chance to grasp their individual significance.

Inversely, the TPM POV can show what the antagonist is doing offscreen to stumble the star. It allows us to spend time with every figure to fully understand their quirks and importance to the overall plot and the people around them. This gives us a satisfyingly holistic picture of what's going on that the other perspectives don't offer.

The third-person multiple POV gives writers the breathing room and flexibility to show their audience how and why their characters fit together like puzzle pieces, and they do well to take advantage of the opportunity it gives them to develop several compelling figures within a single work.

CHARACTER DEVELOPMENT

As *Hunger Games, Divergent, The Fault in Our Stars,* and *To All the Boys I Loved Before* fans will tell you, the protagonist's supporting cast makes the books worth reading. The secondary characters' lively personalities resonate well with audiences, in many cases more than the star themselves does. These first-person accounts do an excellent job animating the supporting cast, but we only get a limited understanding of these figures' inner workings. Secondary characters exist within the context of the protagonist's life, so we don't get to interact with them when they're no longer on the FPN's mind.

With the third-person multiple point of view, we have the freedom to break away from the main plotline to focus on the hero's companions. This perspective gives us insights into the characters' inner musings, motivations, and knowledge that a protagonist is blind to or otherwise disinterested in. The beauty of this perspective is that everyone can be the hero of their own subplot, even if they're not the overall star of the show. It's a great choice for authors who want to write supporting characters with dynamic, well-thought-out backgrounds without making that figure the protagonist. The opposite is also true.

For those of us creatives who have a hard time picking favorites, the TPM POV is the cure-all perspective since it allows each character an equal piece of the action and the audience's attention. In cases like these, there doesn't have to be a single lead. Authors can instead decide to have a constellation of characters that move the story along. Each character's unique experience and personality add an interesting twist to the narrative, especially when it comes to multifaceted plot lines and conflicts.

APPROACH TO SETTING

As mentioned during the onset of this chapter, two people can have drastically different takes on the same event due to their varied ideologies and pasts. The same thing applies to settings. Authors often use the TPM POV to highlight the range of experiences one can have within a space. If you were to pick two people at random from the same city, you'd likely get completely different opinions on and anecdotes about the area. Each character's personality and interests would draw out a unique set of details about the setting and introduce readers to a new subculture within that space. Take my older brother Sean and me, for example.

Despite our small age gap and identical rearing, we have comically different memories of our hometown. As an indoorsy bookworm, I had no interest in going outside unless it was for a high school football game or the annual carnival. To date, don't ask me where things are or what to do; I can't help you because I can't even help myself.

Sean, on the other hand, actually likes that whole going outside thing, so he spent his free time adventuring and skating around with his friends. He'd be able to give you more insights about the area than I ever could because his hobbies allowed him to learn it well. Even though nearly all our biographical and demographic details are the same, our varied interests guarantee that we have different memories of the community we grew up in.

The same concept applies to settings in fiction writing. This narration approach is perfect for giving people a close read into small towns, neighborhoods, and houses. The TPM POV expands these intimate settings to show how many moving pieces, personalities, and subcultures can fit into a tight space and exemplify just how interconnected our lives are.

This concept also applies to stories that take place across bigger venues such as large cities, countries, and continents. Every character's occupation, personal history, disposition, and hobbies play a role in how they interact with their setting, which in turn affects how they shape other figures' lives and the plot at large.

WORLD BUILDING

I've nicknamed the TPM POV the Sightseeing Perspective because it's suited for authors who have worlds worth touring. While the first and second-person POVs are centered around the protagonist's location, the TPM POV allows writers to trapeze around their fictional universe with ease. Readers get to explore the grandeur of the book's different settings far beyond what the main character gets to see, allowing us to flip through the different spectacles like a photo book. Each scene and chapter can take us through a new geographic or sociopolitical spectacle to marvel at, dissect, and connect to other parts of the story.

The TPM perspective is arguably the best for showing off how each setting affects another. It allows authors to explore the various venues within their world without being limited to one character's experience as they would be if they wrote in the first- or second-person point of view. For example, a TPM narrator can show how the different castes of society are interdependent on each other by showing how a farm fire on one planet caused a food drought in a lunar colony that depends on the farm for produce.

Lest the protagonist travels to both places, a first, second, and/or third-person limited narrator could only give readers an intimate understanding of the effects of one of the two affected regions. The TPM POV, on the other hand, can show how the disasters affect the lives of several families, business owners, and farmers, giving us a more thorough understanding of what's happening while also teaching us about new areas.

By allowing authors to give their audience a more in-depth tour of their expansive settings and societies, the TPM POV grants writers the freedom to showcase their work's complex social, political, financial, and interpersonal systems.

The Secret Adversary

People are products of their social and physical environments. Our inner circles shape who we are, how we think, and the way we interact with others. Third-person multiple POV is well suited to represent this phenomenon because it allows authors to show how characters' shared and learned habits influence their personalities and decisions. One fitting example of this is Agatha Christie's novel *The Secret Adversary* (1922).

Christie's book follows amateur detectives and childhood friends Tuppence and Tommy as they try to find and rescue a kidnapped woman. The duo parts ways to follow different leads early on in the plot and remain out of contact until the last few chapters. This separation results in a handful of riveting adventures that showcase their base personalities and influence on one another.

Tuppence has a flair for the dramatic and enjoys the theatrical aspects of detective work. Inversely, Tommy finds acting and espionage stressful. Christie masterfully uses the third-person multiple POV to let them exercise their individuality while showing how their time together impacts the decisions they make. Take Tuppence's attitude toward their mission compared with Tommy's, for example:

> Five minutes later she smiled contentedly at her reflection in the glass. With an actress's pencil she had slightly altered the line of her eyebrows, and that, taken in conjunction with the new luxuriant growth of fair hair above, so changed her appearance that she felt confident that even if she came face to face with Whittington he would not recognize her. She would wear elevators in her shoes, and the cap and apron would be an even more valuable disguise. From hospital experience she knew only too well that a nurse out of uniform is frequently unrecognized by her patients . . .

> The morning brought a note from Mr. Carter:

> "DEAR MISS TUPPENCE,

> "You have made a splendid start, and I congratulate you. I feel, though, that I should like to point out to you once more the risks you are running . . .

> "May I be permitted a word or two of advice? Stick as near to the truth as possible—it minimizes the danger of 'slips.' I suggest that you should represent yourself to be what you are . . .

> Tuppence's spirits rose mercurially. Mr. Carter's warnings passed unheeded. The young lady had far too much confidence in herself to pay any heed to them.

With some reluctance she abandoned the interesting part she had sketched out for herself. Although she had no doubts of her own powers to sustain a role indefinitely, she had too much common sense not to recognize the force of Mr. Carter's arguments.

The young lady's love for acting leads her to treat the mission like a game, focusing on her makeover instead of the threat at hand. Tuppence's affinity for overconfidence and theatrics often led her astray during her childhood, but after years of Tommy telling her that her "[f]ull marks for industry, zero for modesty" would lead to her ruin, she humbles herself enough to accept other people's input.

This passage is a subtle show of his influence on her actions and would have undoubtedly gone unnoticed if it weren't for Christie's choice of perspectives. By opening the novel with their conversation about Tuppence's self-assurance and need for modesty then separating the two, we get to see just how much the dramatist takes his words to heart.

Tommy's time with his best friend influences his solo adventures just as much as his presence impacts hers. While Tuppence has to refer to Tommy's reserved example throughout the text, he has to draw on her theatrics to survive. He models his speech after hers to get out of a sticky situation, though the improvisation brings him nothing but dread, as you can see:

His manner was nonchalant to the last degree. Tommy Beresford was one of those young Englishmen not distinguished by any special intellectual ability, but who are emphatically at their best in what is known as a "tight place."

> Their natural diffidence and caution fall from them like a glove. Tommy realized perfectly that in his own wits lay the only chance of escape, and behind his casual manner he was racking his brains furiously . . .
>
> Tommy was pleased with the concluding words of this speech. His only regret was that Tuppence was not present to appreciate its full flavour.

The TPM POV is often used to show readers how the company that characters keep impacts the way they navigate life. People influence one another, and their relationships affect the way they react to situations. Tommy picked up Tuppence's talent for keeping a straight face and thinking on his feet, but his inner discourse still reflects his adversity to such activities. Had *The Secret Adversary* been narrated from any other perspective, the last line would have fallen flat because we wouldn't have been able to fully understand how much her love and dedication to acting taught him about the craft.

The TPM POV is well suited for authors who are interested in showing how their characters influence one another in a similar fashion. Just as Christie used Tommy and Tuppence's relationship to highlight how people rub off on each other, writers can use this perspective to provide examples of the ways associates affect the way we navigate situations.

Incipience Third-Person Multiple

———

Good versus evil stories are as plentiful and easily consumed as sweets in a candy shop because they're entertaining and predictable. Readers know that they will have a hero to root for, a villain to hate, and a satisfying ending to look forward to. This trend has been upheld for centuries because we rarely get to see things from the antagonist's perspective. The figure's anonymity makes their downfall more satisfying since—more often than not—we don't care about them as individuals because we're not meant to.

The third-person multiple POV allows writers to complicate that relationship by splitting the narrative between the protagonist and antagonist. By presenting the villain's intentions, motivations, and rationale, authors can humanize their evil-doers to the point that their audience feels ambivalent about the figure's fate. In most cases, it's hard not to empathize with someone you've spent time with, so even if readers don't agree with what the antagonist does, they can't help feeling a dash of pity for their fate, especially when many of their traits overlap with the protagonist's.

This TPM rendition of *Incipience* follows Second Recruit Míkuvyo and Izedi Louise during the firefight. Though the Quinzentenian would be considered the bad guy of the scene, her motivations are understandable, and her personality aligns with Louise's so well that she's hard to (completely) hate.

MÍKUVYO

Míkuvyo didn't graduate in second place at the academy just to be benched during the most exciting boarding mission in months. She tries to convince Captain Minókyt to let her serve with the strike and extraction team, but the older woman says she only wants the best of the best for this particular rendezvous. Míkuvyo argues that she fits the bill given her training stats, but her commanding officer tells her that until she proves herself in a real battle, she doesn't qualify. Apparently, simulation scores are only enough to get you placed on a ship but are useless when it comes to mission selection.

Commander Unrok, the veteran soldier responsible for turning new cadets into career soldiers, strikes a deal with the captain to get Míkuvyo and her fellow recruits onboard. He promises to keep the young adults out of sight and in line if they're allowed to observe the operation. Minókyt begrudgingly agrees and stations the group in the cafeteria of all places.

Unlike the rest of her teammates, Míkuvyo doesn't find the humans very amusing, so she talks to the others to pass the time, but even that doesn't do much to stave off the boredom. It takes a few hours for her day to take a turn for the better.

She looks over just in time to see Commander Unrok smack Poním for setting off a laser. Her bored expression softens into a content grin. She loves when the lazy genius gets reprimanded. Each of his mistakes brings her a step closer to replacing him as First Recruit.

If that interaction wasn't enough to put a pep in her step, what happens soon after certainly is. She doesn't know what possesses Unrok to break his promise to the captain by firing on the Inovarian, but she's glad he does. Míkuvyo knows that if she does well here, she might be able to talk her way onto the strike team. Oh, she can taste the prestige now.

She shoots down one human and is aiming at her second by the time her fellow cadets (including Poním!) snap out of their stupor. She can't see their faces due to the invisibility cloaks, but she imagines they wore a dumbfounded expression during those few moments. When she's number one, she'll teach her subordinates a thing or two about staying on their toes.

Míkuvyo makes it a point to hit each of her targets in their right thigh. When the dust settles, she wants a way to distinguish her shots from the others in case Captain Minókyt needs proof of her accomplishments. She zeroes in on this task, flipping between ceiling rafters to get the best angle and only firing when she does. Her efforts yield five incapacitating blows to five victims (if she can even call them that. She is holding back, after all. Captain made it clear that the invalids get to live).

In her determination to be the best marksman, Míkuvyo forgets that she is also a target. She raises her weapon to take down one Earthling when a different one shoots her. Shock registers before the pain does.

The laser eats through her armor, skin, flesh, and bone in the blink of an eye. It cauterizes the blood vessels it licks on the way out, but the impact of her fall bursts them open. The residual heat of the energy blast is enough to make the trickling blood bubble. Míkuvyo clutches her chest to stop the bleeding.

She hears a loud *bang!* followed by the hiss of gas. She looks up in time to see Poním and Unrok escaping. Curses run rampant through her pain-muddled mind. Of course he'd be the one to get out of this unscathed.

LOUISE

A born and raised Georgia peach, Louise knows a thing or two about handling a gun. She can stick a buck from one hundred yards away, and she's damn proud of the bear she snagged the last time she went stalking through the woods with her PeePaw. She can shoot like nobody's business because she was raised to do so, which is why these Quinzentenians and Miss Peace-Lovin Pagi are so frustrating.

Unlike any bobcat, turkey, or possum she's ever hunted, these aliens are agile enough to dodge her shots mid-air and have the means to fight back. Every time she gets one of the elusive buggers in her crosshairs, they trapeze out of the way like some sort of circus freak and send a laser her way for her efforts. Their aim is better than hers so she has to do a lot of ducking and dodging to stay alive while they swing around like it's a playground.

The ability disparity doesn't make her want to give up; it does just the opposite, really. Summoning her Southern stubbornness, Louise pulls out nearly every trick in her hat just to nick one of them. She cheers to herself for a moment, but pride fizzles out faster than a forgotten soda can once she realizes that it's comparatively unimpressive.

The scratch would've been an accomplishment if the Princess Pagi performing *Swan Lake: The Shoot Out* was with her actual team where she was meant to be. The other teen backflips when she should duck and essentially pirouettes to return fire when any normal person would just turn. Her ridiculous antics work well, though, since she's snagged not one but *two* Quinzentenians.

Louise takes aim at one of the three remaining enemies, determined not to be shown up. Normally, another's success wouldn't bother her, but you know what they say: jealousy only bears fruit when inconvenient. Princess Pacifist—and yes, she knows her name—has been against training to help the Inovarians (who helped humans first!) from the very beginning, so her sudden gung ho, "Let's get 'em, boys!" attitude is irritatingly off brand and insulting to those who have been giving it their all since day one.

The huntress has the Quinzentenian swinging through the air in her sight when the lady is thrown off course with a blood-curdling scream. She lands on a downed Izedi before sliding to the ground. Louise doesn't have to look to see who shot her target, but she does anyway.

There she stands in all her pristine glory: Miss Hypocrite and her smoking gun.

Louise resists the urge to scream at her stolen opportunity. Oh, that girl makes her buzz like a rattled box of hornets!

HOW IT'S CHANGED

The third-person multiple POV allows authors to play devil's advocate. Unless the protagonist and the antagonist have a history together, readers don't get many glimpses into the villain's life in works that only follow one character. The absence of these insights makes us form a deeper connection with the hero by default, whereas the introduction of their opposition draws us into the conflict itself.

By giving the Quinzentenians a voice, I've eliminated the aliens' anonymity and created a more interactive reading experience. Even if my readers don't care for Míkuvyo, they're prompted to think about how she feels about her downfall, whereas the original version of *Incipience* considers how the alien's injury makes Mali feel. That is the beauty of this perspective!

Authors may not seek to justify their antagonists' actions or get their readers to side with them, but by giving them experiences to react to, they're guaranteeing that the villain presents as a complex figure that doesn't exist just to goad the protagonist. This humanizing effect is also useful for authors who want to highlight the similarities of their opposing forces.

Míkuvyo and Louise are much more alike than they are dissimilar. They both harbor jealousy for one of their blasé teammates, resent said figure's skills in one way or another, and wish to surpass them. These circumstances motivate them to try their best to shoot down their opponents. I used this perspective to tell their stories because it's perfect for drawing parallels.

The TPM POV allows writers to present characters from various backgrounds and personalities reacting to the same scenario in a way that makes an argument. This duo serves as a fitting example that combatants can view one another as faceless targets who they fail to empathize with when their primary objective is skewed. While this message can be conveyed from a first or third limited narrative, it resonates the best from this perspective since you get to see the extent that both sides exhibit this behavior.

Authors who are interested in widening the scope of their story to teach such lessons and give their antagonists more depth should consider using the third-person multiple point of view since it allows them to explore the multifaceted nature of conflict.

Third Omniscient POV

Fun fact: many authors have a slight God complex. Given the way we spend our days, it certainly makes sense. It's inexplicably satisfying to create universes, fill them with characters, and orchestrate riveting (mis)adventures for them to complete, so it's only fitting to have a perspective that mirrors this power that creatives possess.

DEFINITION

A story narrated in the third-person omniscient (TPO) POV is told by an all-knowing figure who has access to every character's internal discourse and possesses absolute knowledge about the plot's happenings. Their abundance of information allows them to provide the audience with intricate assessments of characters, settings, and conflicts that are unbeknownst and, at times, irrelevant to the other types of narrators. This access to information allows readers to get a holistic view of all the characters' interactions rather than being overly biased because onlookers were limited to one person's experience.

SCOPE

The TPO POV is essentially the upgraded version of the TPM perspective. The two give authors the ability to follow several characters, explore different settings, and show how people's lives are interconnected. They paint the same general picture, but omniscient speakers present it in high definition.

While TPM narratives typically follow one figure per section or chapter, TPO works allow writers to flow between everyone's thoughts in a scene to reveal much more information about the cast at once than the TPM can. This quickly personalizes each figure, establishes character dynamics, and identifies conflicting and parallel interests within a short space to create an exciting reading experience.

TENSION

TPO POV works arguably produce the most exciting dramatic irony because readers get to see how the characters' misunderstandings, miscommunication, and ignorance affect their relationships in real time. Take "The Gift of the Magi" (1905) by O. Henry, for example.

A couple wants to surprise each other with memorable Christmas gifts, so they both secretly sell their most precious items to afford something spectacular for their spouse. The narrator's transitions between their thoughts generate tension for the reader that the characters don't experience. While they're oblivious to their spouse's actions, we're wondering how they'll react once they realize that their gifts are mutually useless.

The TPO POV is perfect for authors who would like to create a dynamic between the audience and the narrative. By presenting the character's emotions and internal dialogue in such an interwoven manner, writers can characterize their figures well and give their readers an emotional scene to anticipate. This tension works well with heartwarming, family-centered short stories like "The Gift of the Magi" and for thrilling mysteries too.

TPONs have the freedom to explicitly tell readers that something atrocious is going to happen to the main character then omit how the figure encounters their fate. This foreknowledge creates a sense of suspense because we know what's in store for them but don't know how they'll get there or react to the situation. This differential is great for creating interactive texts. Oftentimes, people read TPO stories very carefully to pick out the subtle foreshadowing and hints left by the author so they can solve the mystery before the answer is revealed.

WORLD BUILDING

In the other points of view, readers only know as much as the characters do. They may learn what will happen before the cast does via foreshadowing, but by the end of the story, everyone's on the same page. With a TPO narrative, authors have the freedom to provide the audience with information that the characters shouldn't feasibly know. This is true for the perspective at large, but it's especially useful for exploring the complicated settings and social structures found in speculative fiction.

TPOs' all-knowing commentary allows authors to dazzle their audience with their world-building skills. In many cases, it feels inorganic when a protagonist monologues about their setting unless they have a specific reason for listing every detail, so some writers use the TPO POV to have the wiggle room to describe their layout at length.

This narration approach gives authors the freedom to go on asides that explain what the location's climate, topography, technology, cultural history, etc. are like between the protagonists' adventures. This information can be nonessential to the overall plot, but it does help the speculative space feel tangible and enhances the reading experience so the audience feels rooted in the prose.

This perspective helps readers navigate fictional settings and simplifies otherwise complicated discussions. Just as there are thousands of languages on Earth, there can be a handful of fictional vernaculars within a work. This dash of diversity can be equally exciting and frustrating because while it's impressive to see the extent of that world, it can be tiring to read about constant miscommunications.

Speculative fiction writers often make sense of the language barriers through universal translators, spells, and translation mediums when working with other perspectives, but TPOs simplify those interactions by relaying the character's thoughts to the audience. This allows us to see how they navigate their differences while getting the full scope of the conversation.

The third-person omniscient POV is perfect for authors who want to reveal the full extent of their narratives. This perspective gives writers the freedom to flow between their characters' thoughts, showcase their world-building skills, and have fun building a unique dynamic between their none-the-wiser cast and knowledgeable audience.

"Mrs. Spring Fragrance"

———

The third-person omniscient POV is perfect for representing the complexity of relationships. Even the most well-meaning individuals accidentally hurt their loved ones due to inefficient or lacking communication. A prime example of this can be found in "Mrs. Spring Fragrance" (1912) by Sui Sin Far.

This short story follows Mr. and Mrs. Spring Fragrance, a young Chinese couple living in the United States, during their two weeks apart. Mr. Spring Fragrance overhears a snippet of his wife's conversation with their neighbor that leads to an unfortunate misunderstanding.

> Now the only person who knew that Kai Tzu loved Laura and that Laura loved Kai Tzu, was Mrs. Spring Fragrance. The reason for this was that . . . the Chin Yuen parents . . . had betrothed their daughter, Laura, at the age of fifteen, to the eldest son of the Chinese Government school-teacher in San Francisco. The time for the consummation of the betrothal was approaching.

Laura was with Mrs. Spring Fragrance and Mrs. Spring Fragrance was trying to cheer her . . .

"Now, Little Sister," comforted Mrs. Spring Fragrance, "you really must not grieve like that. Is there not a beautiful American poem written by a noble American named Tennyson, which says:

"'Tis better to have loved and lost,

Than never to have loved at all?"

Mrs. Spring Fragrance was unaware that Mr. Spring Fragrance, having returned from the city, tired with the day's business, had thrown himself down on the bamboo settee on the veranda, and that although his eyes were engaged in scanning the pages of the *Chinese World*, his ears could not help receiving the words which were borne to him through the open window . . .

Not wishing to hear more of the secret talk of women, he arose and sauntered around the veranda to the other side of the house.

As anyone who's had their feelings hurt by eavesdropping can tell you, even the most innocent lines can cause immeasurable damage when taken out of context. Since she didn't tell her husband about the teen's romance, Mr. Spring Fragrance doesn't have the background information needed to understand his wife's words and intentions, which leads him to overthink them for the rest of the plot. He eventually draws the false conclusion that his wife's words refer to her own mourning over a lover she had before their arranged marriage or that she's found since then.

The beauty of the third-person omniscient point of view is that we aren't subjected to the same confusion. This narration style gives us a split-screen view of the plot that allows us to inhabit multiple spaces and conversations at once. Our informed position as readers gives us a better understanding of the premise, conflict, and characters than that of the protagonists. This knowledge not only orients us in the text but also creates a mood that is independent of the Spring Fragrances' experiences.

Far uses the TPO perspective to create three atmospheres in her short story: Mr. Spring Fragrance's melancholy space, his wife's euphoric bubble, and the audience's amused vantage point. The prose's tone shifts between the husband's decline and his spouse's cheer so often that his misery is comical. Though the narration around his experience is somber, readers aren't inclined to fully empathize with his woes because we know they're a fabrication of his imagination. Take the following scene, for example.

Mr. Spring Fragrance, still confused by the Tennyson quote, asks his American friend how marriage works in the States to get more context. The young man tells him that love comes before the wedding, so there's no guarantee that doing things backward (according to Western culture) would result in mutual affection. Before we can settle into his sorrowful mourning of his own arranged marriage, Far's TPON provides us with this juxtaposition to lighten the mood:

> . . . it rankled in his mind as he entered the telegraph office. If his wife was becoming as an American woman, would it not be possible for her to love as an American woman—a man to whom she was not married? There also floated in his memory the verse which his wife had quoted to the daughter of Chin Yuen. When

the telegraph clerk handed him a blank, he wrote this message:

"Remain as you wish, but remember that "Tis better to have loved and lost, than never to have loved at all.""

When Mrs. Spring Fragrance received this message, her laughter tinkled like falling water. How droll! How delightful! Here was her husband quoting American poetry in a telegram. Perhaps he had been reading her American poetry books since she had left him! She hoped so. They would lead him to understand her sympathy for her dear Laura and Kai Tzu . . . Strange that that should be so, since he had fallen in love with her picture before *ever* he had seen her, just as she had fallen in love with his! And when the marriage veil was lifted and each beheld the other for the first time in the flesh, there had been no disillusion—no lessening of the respect and affection, which those who had brought about the marriage had inspired in each young heart.

Mrs. Spring Fragrance began to wish she could fall asleep and wake to find the week flown, and she in her own little home pouring tea for Mr. Spring Fragrance.

This scene summarizes the couple's situation so well that the disparity is humorous. Tennyson's quote is both Mr. Spring Fragrance's cinder block shoes and the wind beneath his counterpart's wings. Those two well-meaning lines cause the man to grieve his wife's allegedly unreciprocated affections while she falls deeper in love with him because he finally understands her (which is ironic in every sense of the word). This immaculate scene's resonance would have been impossible to compose in any other perspective.

The TPM POV, the only other technique that could facilitate this narrative, would have required definitive breaks between their commentary that would have completely changed the scene's impact. The section could be rewritten from both spouse's perspectives to give a fair representation of their emotions, but this approach would make them feel more like opposing forces rather than a team that is a conversation away from mutual contentment.

Thankfully, Sui Sin Far decided to write this slice-of-life piece in the TPO perspective, which allowed her to construct a dramatic yet heartwarming tale. Authors who are interested in creating one-sided tension from ideal circumstances do well to take notes from her. Far does an excellent job of showing how innocent misunderstandings, the bread and butter of the TPO POV, can be life changing for one, insignificant for another, and entertaining for the audience.

While Mr. Spring Fragrance is in a tizzy over inaccurate information, we get the chance to chuckle at his antics because we understand his relationship better than he does. By flowing between the couple's thoughts throughout the story, the TPON allows us to witness their mutual affection and see how it influences their daily lives. This not only characterizes the pair in an endearing manner but also raises the stakes for the climax.

Mr. and Mrs. Spring Fragrance had a spotless relationship before the Tennyson quote was introduced, so readers are curious to know whether it will remain that way upon her return home. As we approach the apex, Mrs. Spring Fragrance grows exponentially more excited to see her husband while he's increasingly anxious at the thought of interacting with her. This bout revs up the dramatic irony and pulls us into the plot. The rising tension makes us eager to read the ending because their reunion may solve the questions that we desperately need answered, such as:

- Will he confront her upon her return home?

- Does she ever find out that he eavesdropped?

- Will she get a chance to explain herself?

- Will he ever be able to recover from his heartbreak?

- Are they going to be okay?

These are just a few of the questions that keep readers turning the page. Even though we know how these characters feel about each other, there is no guarantee that their reunion will go well because this one miscommunication turned Mr. Spring Fragrance on his head. That is the appeal of the TPO POV. It is perfect for authors who want to entertain their readers with the chaotic nature of communication because it allows them to show just how quickly minor misunderstandings can avalanche into life-changing issues.

Incipience Third-Person Omniscient POV

Detectives aim to interview every witness at the scene of a crime because they all experienced the travesty from different literal and psychological angles. Their preferences and biases influence what they focus on, so each of their testimonies brings something new to the table. When writing up their report, the investigator curates this information into a single document. The same concept applies to the third-person omniscient point of view.

The TPO perspective lets readers see the plot unfold through every character's eyes. The diction and tone of each figure's account shift as the author briefly inhabits their headspace to show readers the central object and/or person from various angles. In this TPO rendition of *Incipience*, my narrator gives you a 360-degree view of the contributing factors and characters that lead to Mali's first real fight.

THE ORATOR

An eye for an eye leads to a blind world, but the Inovarians and Quinzentenians are comfortable in the dark. Their history of dragging each other down with increasingly vicious retaliative measures has made conflict a part of their daily lives, so much so that they forget that few species are as used to fighting as they are.

The humans trained for months under the Inovarians but are still painfully ill suited and underqualified to participate in this battle. No amount of simulation training could have adequately prepared them for the pain of seeing their comrades cut down and worrying whether the same will happen to them.

The gravity of the situation presses down on their chests. The Izedis, as the Inovarians call these cadets, have the highest scores in artillery and combat simulations. Still, their hands tremble as they aim at their adversaries. The young adults have existed within the safety of Inovarian custody for so long that they forgot that the Quinzentenians are more than holograms from the training room. All of a sudden, they're dodging real lasers, not LED lights. Getting hit now means that they're out in more ways than one.

The better half of the Izedis want to defect for their own safety, but the fear of getting shot in the back during their retreat keeps them rooted in the cafeteria. Well, that and their injuries won't let them get far.

Quinzentenian Captain Minókyt initially forbade her trainees from interacting with the humans, but now that Commander Unrok's long-unresolved flashbacks have made him trigger-happy, nothing is stopping them from toying with the insufficiently trained anthropoids. Second Recruit Míkuvyo wastes no time decorating her targets with her signature leg shot, seeing every mark as an avenue toward promotion.

Many of her comrades view the situation in the same light and shoot to make an impression. First Recruit Poním is the only Quinzentenian who isn't aiming to injure (or kill, in Unrok's case). The expert marksman has nothing to prove and would rather be entertained by the humans' scurrying than put them out of commission. Besides, there is only one target that's worth his time and talent, and he's not foolish enough to pursue her.

Poním calls her Enigma because, among her peers, Charlotte-Amalie is just that. The teen moves with the grace of a Quinzentenian and has reflexes that surpass their own. Her prowess and talent for instant retaliation are enough to deter Poním—after all, there's no prize for subduing her—and are noteworthy enough to pique Minókyt's interests.

From the safety of her ship, the captain can't help but be impressed by the girl's talents. Given her comrades' lackluster performances, Minókyt is certain that Charlotte-Amalie's abilities are unique to her, though she cannot determine why. The human's movements are far too fluid to be the result of the Stiffs' tutelage, and her fighting style seems dependent on her instincts, not intelligence. (If they were, the captain realizes, her targets would be dead instead of injured).

Minókyt rises from her station. There's only so much to be learned from a ship away. She'd like to see the girl in action herself.

Unbeknownst to her, Charlotte-Amalie has attracted the attention of her enemies and allies alike. Izedi Reese is in awe of her innate talent for combat, impressed that she's developed such a destructive style of her own during their time onboard. Cadet Louise, embarrassed to be shown up by a pacifist, finds herself working twice as hard to compete with her. Even Commander Rombag, who has always known what she can do, is surprised by the extent of his student's abilities.

Whether she realizes it or not, Charlotte-Amalie is responsible for the majority of Quinzentenian injuries since her commander has been occupied with Unrok's incessant attacks. Rombag believes that if she decided to fully commit herself to the Inovarian army, she would be the most formidable warrior in its recent history. He truly hopes that will be the case, but he knows her too well to hold his breath for it.

His cadet is a naturally vengeful creature with too much empathy to use her talents for the viciousness war requires. While she may be angry and desperate enough to fight this battle, she doesn't have the resolve to do much more than that.

Across the cafeteria, Charlotte-Amalie bites back vomit after shooting down Míkuvyo. She tries to numb her mind to the results of her actions. Any other soldier would have been proud of the impressive blow, but she reels at the thought of placing someone else—enemy or not—on death's door.

Poním and Unrok escape with a smoke bomb before she can hyperventilate. Once the dust clears, she fixates on the Izedis. Their miserable groans pacify her ailing conscience. These young adults didn't deserve to be caught in the crossfire, nor should their livelihoods have been ripped from them for a fight that was never theirs to begin with.

When Commander Rombag asks for volunteers to help rescue the Quinzentenians' other victims, Charlotte-Amalie steps forward without a second thought. She knows an eye for an eye leads to a blind world, but some things are worth wading through the shadows.

HOW IT'S CHANGED

The third-person omniscient POV allows readers to get the full scope of a situation. This narration style flows between different settings and characters' thoughts to provide the most thorough explanation of events possible. *Incipience*'s original style focuses on Mali's individual experience and uses the secondary characters as tools to further the plot. The prose is rooted in her candid thoughts, feelings, and reactions to other characters but gives little consideration to how she affects those figures as well.

The third-person omniscient POV is perfect for authors who enjoy characterizing their protagonists by placing them in group settings. It allows us to see the main character from different angles because each person they interact with notices different details about the figure, which contributes to our understanding of them. Characters rarely exist in a vacuum, so this narration style is well suited to explore how the lead's interactions with others speak to their personalities.

Reasonably, Mali doesn't spend much time on introspection during the firefight, so readers draw their own conclusions about who she is based on what she does. In the TPO rewrite, the other characters do the same thing, but by stating their opinions, I provide a more concrete character profile. For example, Poním identifies Mali as a threat; Minókyt's observations paint the teen as an abnormality, and Rombag's assessments show her talent for war. While the original prose leads readers to these same deductions, the TPO rendition reinforces these traits by explaining how she looks to other characters.

I highly recommend authors sample this perspective if they are interested in developing their protagonists in a similar manner. Just as people are defined by the impact they leave on others, the third-person omniscient point of view can be used to characterize figures by showing how their actions influence those around them.

Dear Reader,

———

Choosing your story's point of view is one of the first and most important decisions you will make while working on your project. Perspective influences every detail of your plot because it determines what narrative techniques, literary conventions, and character types you use. These elements then determine how your audience resonates with the text, so do yourself a favor and choose wisely, and know that you don't have to choose exclusively.

Contrary to popular belief, you're not limited to one point of view per project. Creative writing is constantly expanding to embrace new storytelling tactics, and one such innovation is hybrid narratives. These works use multiple perspectives to change the text's diction, tone, and mood to provide a unique experience for readers. Sample your prose in each perspective to see what suits your goals the best, and mix and match if you believe that hybrid narration will execute your plot as desired. Whether you choose to adhere to classical conventions or innovate alongside your contemporaries, make it a point to understand what the power of point of view can do for you.

Cheers to the projects to come!

Kristin S. Smith

Acknowledgments

___

It takes a village to raise a child and a few more to publish a book. I'd like to thank the creative, personal, and professional communities that helped support me throughout this process. They repeatedly forced me to spit out the negativity and self-doubt that I was determined to swallow and then spoon-fed me nothing but love and positivity in its wake.

Thank you to the following creatives and small business owners who helped me champion my imposter syndrome with their words of wisdom and inspired me with their own success:

Zachary Sclafani (Actor, @ zach_sclafani on Instagram), Arbishua Rojas (Clothing Brand CEO, @ nerd.sq on Instagram), Arlene Sutton (Jeweler, @ angelaura on Instagram), John North (Author, @ omniwrites on Instagram), Michael Taylor (Fashion Designer, @ taylorantonio_ on IG), Imani Benjamin (Writer, @ mani_morning on Instagram), Carolyn Skowron (Author, @ carolyn.skowron on Instagram), Chip Robinson (Director, @ cult.francis on Instagram), Haley Toolsie (Digital Creator, @ haleytoolsie), David Hazward Jr (Graphic Designer, @ _speccs_ on Instagram), Alexis Vega (Cosmetologist, @alexis.cosmetology on Instagram), Eric Koester (CEO of Creators Institute, @ erickoester on IG),

Kelly (Author, @fictionleisure on Instagram), Seth Kwesi Kumi (Founder of United Stoles Limited, @ UnitedStoles on Instagram), (Gregory Morris, (gkmorrismd on LinkedIn), Olivia Harden (Journalist, @ livineuphoria on Twitter), John Adcox (Author and CEO of Gramarye Media, @ JohnAdcox and @ GramaryeMedia on Twitter), and Cassidy Hayes (Owner of Pins 'n Paper Editing Services).

Thank you to my wonderful family, friends, and mentors for lavishing me with love, encouragement, and well-wishes from the moment I announced this project. I lost count of how many hugs, pep talks, and words of encouragement I received, but I will never forget the warmth they all brought me.

Randy Smith Jr, Denise See, Randy Smith Sr, Lynnette Smith, Kole Smith, Kevin Smith, Sean Smith, Marissa Smith, Gaby Smith, Danilyn Banaban, Ena Smith, Renecia Wilson, Emerald Mcneal, Cherie J Arnold, Ruddy Smith, Ruby Smith Bass, Roselyn Dawes, Ronna Wade, Monique Liburd, Andrew Khong, Autumn Lundblad, Brittaney Vargas, Nancy Her, Miah Earl, Allyson B Ault, Norman D. Ault, Kelly Boatman, Ian M Young, Matthew Centofranchi, Jordan King, Gavin Garcia, Kamille Pryce, Garrett Johnson, Matthew Smith, Ashley Hoagland, Chris Jacobs, Paxton Owen Freeman, Miranda Mccallum, Jacob Garcia, Sydney Steiger, Trudy Chase , Rebecca Rios, Timothy Stepney, Jalen Mitchell, Mike Emanuel Santiago, Megan Cintron, Ramon Saldana, Cher Smith, Allison Renslow, Candace New, Delaney C, Amber Woods, Summer Brown, Nidhi Gangavarapu, Maréva Baïkoua, Juliet Penna, Lindsay Ferren, Danielle Hawthorne, Adriane L Davis, Karina Whamond, Cammeo Lucía Lea Gaviota, Edidiong Etokudo, Alina Baron, Dolly Ukpong, Levi Norte, Autumn Collins, Veronica Leon-Solis, LiLi

Orange, Timothy Stepney. Jean Dibgolongo. Cassidye Devers, Michelle Lee, Jeff Steely, Kalynn Perez, Garrett Johnson, Emily Brannen, Michael Taylor, Kalysta Seyini Combs Henderson, Imani Denise Armour, Micayla Mueller, Obdulia Jimenez, Brittany l, Allyson Stephens, Alexys Campbell, Hannah Perez, Winter Lake, Serenity Jackson, Cassandra Ogletree, Ron Boatman, Liliana Rodriguez, Cathy Henderson, Andrea Lacey, Catherine Sum, Esequiel Isaiah Escobedo, Rebecca Rios, Roxann Smith, Dylan O'Dell, Erika R, Emily Moreno, Aileen Morales, Isabel Duran, Andrea Padilla.

Last but certainly not least, thank you to Eric Koester, Mike Butler, Alan Zatkow, and the staff of New Degree Press for helping me complete this fulfilling project. Professor Koester's Creator Institute started me down this path by innovating my writing as my developmental editor Mike Butler enthusiastically showed me how to turn my POV anecdote into a manuscript. I would like to give a special thank-you to my phenomenal marketing and revisions editor, Alan Zatkow, for hefting me out of the pits of my self-doubt (and procrastination) more times than I can count. Without his patience, encouragement, and humor-laced advice, neither I nor this book would be anywhere near as refined as we are today.

Appendix

FIRST-PERSON PROTAGONIST

Green, John. *The Fault in Our Stars.* New York: Penguin Group, 2012.

Poe, Edgar A. *The Works of Edgar Allan Poe,* vol. 2. Urbana: The Project Gutenberg, 2020. https://www.gutenberg.org/files/2148/2148-h/2148-h.htm#chap2.11

FIRST-PERSON SECONDARY

Melville, Herman. *Moby-Dick; Or the Whale.* Urbana: Project Gutenberg, 2001. https://www.gutenberg.org/files/2701/2701-h/2701-h.htm.

FIRST-PERSON UNRELIABLE

Gilman, Charlotte Perkins. "The Yellow Wallpaper." Urbana: Project Gutenberg, 2021. https://www.gutenberg.org/files/1952/1952-h/1952-h.htm

Morrison, Toni. "Recitatif." In The Norton Anthology of American Literature, edited by Robert S. Levine, 1429–42. New York: W.W. Norton & Company, 2007.

Poe, Edgar A. The Works of Edgar Allan Poe, vol. 2. Urbana: Project Gutenberg, 2020. https://www.gutenberg.org/files/2148/2148-h/2148-h.htm#chap2.20.

Rae, Haniya. "When Poison Was Everywhere." The Atlantic, October 11, 2016. https://www.theatlantic.com/health/archive/2016/10/the-era-when-poison-was-everywhere/503654/.

FIRST-PERSON OBSERVER
Doyle, Arthur Conan. *The Case-Book of Sherlock Holmes.* Urbana: Project Gutenberg, 2016. http://gutenberg.net.au/ebooks01/0100291h.html#ref09.

SECOND PERSON
Hawthorne, Nathaniel. *Twice Told Tales.* Urbana: Project Gutenberg, 2017. https://www.gutenberg.org/files/13707/13707-h/13707-h.htm#haunted.

Rey, Tanya. "Blooming." *The Sun,* October 2020. https://www.thesunmagazine.org/issues/538/blooming.

THIRD-PERSON LIMITED
Chopin, Kate. "The Story of an Hour." Accessed August 20, 2021. https://www.katechopin.org/story-hour/.

THIRD-PERSON MULTIPLE
Christie, Agatha. *The Secret Adversary.* Urbana: Project Gutenberg, 2019. https://www.gutenberg.org/cache/epub/1155/pg1155-images.html.

Marlon, James. *A Brief History of Seven Killings.* New York: Riverhead Books, 2014.

Orange, Tommy. *There There*. New York: Alfred A. Knopf, 2018.

THIRD-PERSON OMNISCIENT

Far, Sui Sin. *Mrs. Spring Fragrance*. Urbana: Project Gutenberg, 2020. https://www.gutenberg.org/files/7256/7256-h/7256-h.htm.

Henry, O. "The Gift of the Magi." Urbana: Project Gutenberg, 2015. https://www.gutenberg.org/files/7256/7256-h/7256-h.htm.